The History of
LONG BEACH POLY

SCHOLARS & CHAMPIONS

To Scott Karres,

Your Poly family misses you!
Thank you for leaving an imprint in
our hearts on Jackrabbit Lane. Can't
wait for you to return home.
Much Jackrabbit love to you!

MIKE GUARDABASCIO & TYLER HENDRICKSON
Foreword by Billie Jean King

THE
History
PRESS

Published by The History Press
Charleston, SC
www.historypress.com

Front cover, top: The front of Long Beach Polytechnic High School, circa 2018. *Photo by Stephen Carr. Bottom*: The old Poly campus, collapsed after the 1933 earthquake. *From Poly historical archives.*

First published 2019

Manufactured in the United States

ISBN 9781467135283

Library of Congress Control Number: 2019943517

For Maya
—Mike

For Mom
—Tyler

CONTENTS

Foreword, by Billie Jean King   9
Introduction   13

1. Early Years, 1895–1911   17
2. New Campus, 1911–1932   25
3. The Earthquake, 1933   35
4. Rebuilding and World War II, 1933–1945   42
5. Postwar Boom, 1946–1966   59
6. Race Riots at Poly, 1967–1972   68
7. Back from the Brink, 1972–1985   79
8. Years of Growth, Centennial, 1986–1995   94
9. Poly the Powerhouse, 1996–Present   104
10. Jackrabbit Traditions   114
11. The Art Museum on the Eastside   121
12. Poly at War   125
13. Trailblazing Jackrabbits in Women's Sports   132
14. Scholars and Champions and Musicians   136
15. Rappers, Singers and Rock Stars   143
16. Fraternities and Sororities at Poly   151
17. PAAL   155
18. Hollywood Poly   157
19. Scholars: PACE and CIC, Poly's Magnets   166
20. Champions: Poly's Sports Programs   175

Contents

Afterword. Green and Gold Forever   189
Acknowledgements   193
Index   197
About the Authors   203

FOREWORD

It's been a few years since I graduated from Long Beach Poly High School, but the lessons that I learned there have stayed with me throughout my life and career. A lot of Moffitts have walked the hallways at Poly. Both my parents, Bill and Betty, and my brother, Randy, are Poly graduates.

When you walk into the school, there's a sign over the entrance that says, "Enter to Learn, Go Forth to Serve." I just loved that as a student; it got me pumped up every day the way a coach gets you inspired.

The other sign when you look up to the left it says, "Home of Scholars and Champions."

At Poly, we love to win CIF titles. We like to win. But being a champion can mean anything, not just sports—you can be a champion in life, too.

Those messages meant a lot to me as a student and they still mean a lot to me today.

What most people don't understand is that when I went to Poly, girls didn't get to win CIF titles. We had to be happy with our Girls' Athletic Association letters, and we could only play at the school against each other. I was leaving every day to go play tennis—we didn't even have a proper tennis team. We didn't get to play in the Moore League when I was in school—now that would have been something.

I will forever be grateful to the teachers, administrators and coaches from my days at Poly. You never do anything alone. Mrs. Johnson was my physical education teacher my senior year. I had offered to give tennis clinics to the other students, and all the previous physical education teachers had said

Billie Jean King's senior mugshot in the 1961 Poly *Caerulea* yearbook. *Courtesy* Caerulea *archives.*

no. Mrs. Johnson said, "They didn't want them? Well, I do." As a senior, she had me do clinics and teach—she understood what I was doing with my tennis career. She was so supportive of me in every way.

A lot has improved since I left Poly. And since Title IX was passed on June 23, 1972, Poly has become a leader in girls' sports. That makes me very proud.

One opportunity I got from Poly that I know students there still get is the chance to learn as part of a diverse community. That really helped all of us. I was in a service sorority called Zayn, and one of my sorority sisters was Japanese—hearing about what her family went through during World War II with the internment camps and hearing stories about what some of our black classmates were going through was eye-opening.

We always talked to each other, and being in sports we all knew each other. Poly had a very successful culture of sports and a legacy of success inside and out of sports. A legacy can be considered pressure, but we felt like it was an opportunity to continue that legacy, to be something that made the school and your family proud.

We all loved going to Poly; we were very clear on our heritage and the legacy we wanted to leave. I'm so glad Mike and Tyler have written this book so that people can learn more about what the school has been through in its history to get to where it is today.

Anywhere I go in the world, people come up to me and talk about Poly. Gene Washington and I would run into each other all the time and be so proud to have gone there. Vania King and I still share Poly stories when we see each other. I met Chase Utley when he was with the Phillies, and we were so happy to say "Go Jackrabbits" to each other. He wanted to know where I went to junior high, and it turned out we both went to Hughes and Poly a trillion years apart—that's the kind of fun you get to have with all the alums all over the world.

What was unique about Poly was we had the richest kids in Long Beach, we had the middle class and we had the poorest kids. I liked being at school with all three; I think we all learned more about the world that way. I was one of the blue-collar kids from the wrong side of the tracks. With all the different kinds of kids coming from all the different backgrounds we had, it was still such a positive place.

I hope that it stays that way. I want them to keep winning and creating young people who are going to be champions in life and scholars. I hope the students keep going forth to serve, to do something in life that's bigger than them as individuals.

Poly provides that spirit and inspiration and gives you insight into so many different cultures. All of that puts you way ahead of anyone else when you graduate.

—Billie Jean King

Billie Jean King is a legend on and off the tennis court. In her playing career, she won 129 titles, including 39 Grand Slam titles. Her win over Bobby Riggs in the Battle of the Sexes television event was watched by 90 million viewers. She's also been a crusader for the rights of women and the LGBTQ community for decades and was the recipient of the Presidential Medal of Freedom in 2009. In 2018, she and partner Ilana Kloss became minority owners of the Dodgers—at their introductory press conference, Dodgers infielder Chase Utley and King interrupted the event to yell "Go Jackrabbits!" to each other. Shortly after this book is published, Long Beach will rename its main library branch as the Billie Jean King Main Library.

INTRODUCTION

Take a walk up Atlantic Avenue on a sunny spring day with us. We're not in the nicest part of Long Beach, California, but we are in perhaps the most famous area, one immortalized by the rise of gangster rap in the 1980s and '90s. Soon we reach Long Beach Polytechnic High School, the oldest institution in the city. Long Beach itself was founded in 1897, but Poly has had its doors open to the city's best and brightest since 1895.

Let's turn and walk toward the school's front gates. We pass Founder's Rock, which was sunk in the ground in front of the original campus 120-plus years ago and brought over to Sixteenth and Atlantic in 1911 when the school moved to this location. We walk past the rock toward the gates, passing under the copper engraving of one of the school's mottos: Enter to Learn, Go Forth to Serve. In the building on our left is a nearly century-old mural, so rare and valuable it's federally protected, encased in glass.

As we pass through the entrance, we turn and look behind us at a freshly painted iteration of one of the school's other mottos: Home of Scholars and Champions. We're now in the quad at the heart of the campus, one that holds thousands of students. In the center of the quad is a flagpole; its base is constructed from columns that were the signature architectural pieces of the campus that stood here before it was leveled by a 1933 earthquake. There's a cornerstone in the base of the flagpole laid more than a century ago.

Stretching through the center of the quad is a rose garden meticulously maintained over the decades. The roses and their thorns represent the beauty of one of America's most diverse and storied schools as well as the hard times it's persevered through. Those times seem far away now, though. It's spring, and the sun is shining on Long Beach Poly.

Today is the Intercultural Fair, one of the most unique traditions at a school that is packed with them—in one form or another, it dates back to 1937's International Good Will Day, when students could buy Japanese, German and French food from one another. In the 1950s, it became the International Carnival, a way of raising money to bring foreign exchange students to the school. Today, the Intercultural Fair is a way for cultural clubs to raise money and for students to appreciate the diversity of their campus, their city and their world.

Lining the edges of the quad are dozens of booths run by the school's students. The smells of every kind of home-cooked food you could imagine become intertwined, filling the air. There are several kinds of barbecue, from Samoan to Korean to Southern. There's Cambodian, Vietnamese and Chinese food, lasagna and pizza, homemade cheesecake and hot links, Nigerian and Native American cuisine—all alongside teriyaki, tacos, brisket, fried rice, greens and empanadas.

All around you, students are lined up to try traditional dishes, laughing and joking with one another. It's an image almost comical in its harmony, a picture of the public school that America wants to send its children to: racially and economically diverse, competitive but nurturing. While the students make their plates, the rally stage hosts a rotating group of entertainment: punk bands, rappers, jazz ensembles and Polynesian, K-pop and folklórico dancers.

Looking at the scene today, it's hard to imagine all the things this school has been through. An earthquake destroyed most of the campus in 1933, forcing Poly to start from scratch. Racial strife and violence threatened to close the campus in the late 1960s and early 1970s.

From the ashes of each disaster, a powerhouse rose in Long Beach's inner city: A school that's produced more NFL and MLB players than any other in America and has won more championships than any other in California. A school with six GRAMMYs to its name as well as dozens of well-known musicians and actors among its alumni ranks who've won GRAMMYs, Emmy Awards and Oscars. A school that's a shining beacon for academics, with more students admitted to the University of California system and the Ivy Leagues than any other public school in the country.

It's a remarkable story, unlike any other in American education, and never before told in its entirety. This work chronicles the story of the school from its founding through all of its ups and downs. We've conducted hundreds

Left: The Intercultural Fair in 1980, looking much the same as it does today. *Courtesy* Caerulea *archives*.

Below: Long Beach Poly's Intercultural Fair today. *Photo by Stephen Carr.*

of interviews with alums, former staffers and education experts to try to give you the fullest picture we could. The first half of the book is a straight history of Poly as an institution, while the second half explores some of the prominent Jackrabbit programs and alums. We also take a closer look at the fascinating lives of lesser-known Poly products (as well as some famous ones) in the Jackrabbit Spotlights scattered throughout.

Before we begin, a quick word on what this book isn't. This is not an encyclopedic listing of all of Poly's famous alumni or an attempt to name-drop every significant person to have passed through the school as a student or employee or coach. Such an enterprise would take up an entire book on its own, and while that might be a worthwhile undertaking, it's not the story we've set out to tell.

What we hope this book is, instead, is the story of how this school and this campus has done something incredible and succeeded in ways no one else has ever been able to. It's the story of a school that's like the rose garden in the quad: a school that's grown through concrete and pushed its way toward the light, blooming into something as rare as it is beautiful.

1

EARLY YEARS, 1895–1911

Long Beach Poly was founded in 1895, two years before the City of Long Beach incorporated. Because the high school is actually older than the city whose name it bears, their stories are intertwined.

In the 1880s, the stretch of beachside land that would become the city had a scant few dozen families living in grouped camps. As more people moved into "town," there was an increasing need for a teacher. The first organized education in Long Beach began in the fall of 1885, as nine school-aged children were taught by sixteen-year-old Grace Bush, who was given seventy-five dollars for her efforts. That was a whopping twenty-five dollars per month for a three-month contract.

With storefronts rapidly going up, the school's original location was to be a new building at Pine Avenue and Second Street—but it was sold two weeks into the school year, so postmaster W.W. Lowe lent the town a tent for Bush to teach in.

As people flooded into the area that is now Downtown Long Beach and a true city began to take shape, money was quickly raised. In 1885, a school bond of $6,000 was passed to fund construction of the Central School at Pine and Sixth Streets, with the land sold at a cheap price by William Willmore, the unofficial founder of Long Beach. In May 1888, another $3,500 bond was passed to fund expansion of the campus. The city still wasn't very big—those two elections had twenty-two and thirty-five voters, respectively. But the young families of Long Beach were already concerned with education.

John Bixby and Belle Lowe were the movers behind a push for the creation of a formalized school district. Lowe, the postmaster's wife, was a mover and shaker who would later be credited as the woman who gave the City of Long Beach its name. The school district was effectively formed on September 3, 1895, when an election was held to determine whether or not Long Beach should start its first high school. The vote was unanimous in favor of that plan, and two weeks later the first incarnation of Long Beach Poly opened.

THE FIRST CLASSES

The plan was to locate the classes at the Central School, but when forty-three students enrolled, it was obvious that a bigger facility would be needed. The first classes of what was then referred to as Long Beach High School convened in the Methodist Tabernacle Chapel at the northeast corner of Third Street and Locust Avenue. That site is now the northern end of the Long Beach Promenade, the home of Harvey Milk Park.

Professor Walter S. Bailey was the first principal of the school, and Hattie Mason Willard was the first teacher for the twenty-one freshmen, fifteen sophomores and seven juniors. Mason Willard had the unenviable task of teaching three levels of English, math, history, Latin, Greek and German to the entire student body. By the end of the year, Harriet Bowles had been brought in to teach the ninth graders and Katharine Mosher was hired to teach Latin. Longtime English teacher Jane Harnett would be hired two years later.

With enrollment growing, the Long Beach Schools Board of Trustees hired Howard L. Lunt in the summer of 1896 to serve as both principal of Long Beach High and supervising head of the entire school district, a job he held for only one year before it was split into two positions.

On June 18, 1897, Ernest Shaul became the first graduate of Long Beach High and the only graduate in the class of '97.

"I have left the harbor," he said in a valedictory speech to the other students at the school. "The ocean is before me."

Class sizes continued to swell rapidly as the city incorporated in 1897 and began to stretch its roots, with a construction boom of hotels and restaurants all over town. Classes moved from the Tabernacle to the Chautauqua Hall at Pine Ave and Fourth Street. The Chautauqua was usually the host of social events like formal dances, but for a year and a half it was the holding pen for Long Beach High's students while the first real campus was being constructed.

In 1897, the citizens of Long Beach passed their third school bond in as many years, this time in the form of a $10,000 bond that would go to build the city's first high school campus at Eighth Street and American Avenue (now Long Beach Boulevard).

Because the city was still so small, there were many who doubted the wisdom of that move, including Los Angeles County's superintendent of schools, Spurgeon Riley, who admitted he had "sincere misgivings" about sleepy Long Beach's ability to fund and support a true high school.

"The mistake I made was in assuming Long Beach to be an ordinary community," said Riley, as quoted in the Long Beach Unified School District's (LBUSD) history of education in the city.

THE FIRST CAMPUS

It was on May 20, 1898, that Long Beach High School officially opened at Eighth and American—not squatting in a church or a social hall, but in its own beautiful Mission-style building with a red tile roof, several classrooms and an assembly hall. It was the first publicly owned building in Long Beach and the first high school in Los Angeles County that was outside the city of Los Angeles.

Although that area is now considered in the thick of things, Long Beach was still so small at the time that the school was referred to as being "way out on the edge of town" by the local newspaper. Currently, the LBUSD operates Renaissance High School at the location, although there's a bronze plaque outside the school acknowledging it as the first location of Long Beach Poly.

From 1898 until 1911, the campus at Eighth and American was home to Long Beach High, and traditions were formed that still last to this day. For one, the school's original color scheme of red and white was thrown out in favor of green and gold in 1899 after a semipro baseball team donated green and gold uniforms to the school's newly established baseball team. Five years later, in 1904, Poly added football and basketball teams. The student-run Long Beach High School Athletic Association was responsible for raising funds and organizing everything to do with the school's sports programs.

That spirit of self-governance was a big part of Long Beach High from the early days. In 1906, the school formed its own student-run

Poly's first campus at what is now the corner of Eighth Street and Long Beach Boulevard. The school was located there until 1911, when it moved to Sixteenth and Atlantic. *Courtesy* Caerulea *archives.*

government, the commission system that's still in use more than a century later. At the time that was a big deal: it was the first student-led government in the state of California.

The city itself continued to grow at a rapid rate. From the dozen or so families who had first pitched their tents in 1885, Long Beach grew to a population of 2,252 at the turn of the century, with 550 pupils enrolled in school. In 1902, Courtney Teel became the first student to graduate from Long Beach High having gone through every grade in Long Beach schools.

The year 1903 saw the publication of the first *Caerulea*, Poly's yearbook. Katherine Mosher, the school's language teacher, served as the yearbook advisor and also gave it the name *Caerulea*, which was meant to evoke the deep blue sea off the Long Beach coast.

One of the first organized activities at the school was a classical orchestra, pictured here in 1909. *Courtesy* Caerulea *archives.*

An early Poly baseball team featuring George Stovall, one of the first Poly baseball players to make it to the Major Leagues. *Courtesy* Caerulea *archives.*

JACKRABBIT SPOTLIGHT: CLYDE DOYLE

Clyde Doyle was among the first group of students to attend Long Beach High School, graduating in 1909 before going on to earn his law degree at USC in 1917. After practicing law in Long Beach, he embarked on a long career of public service. Doyle was charter president of the Long Beach Kiwanis Club and the first president of the Long Beach Boy Scout Council, and he was even director of the YMCA. He received numerous meritorious awards from the Inter-Allied Service Clubs in Long Beach, the Veterans of Foreign Wars, American Legion, American Veterans of World War II and Korea and the Disabled American Veterans.

In 1941, he served as a member of the California State Board of Education and would soon after begin a successful career in politics. Doyle, a Democrat, was elected to the U.S. House of Representatives in 1944, representing California's Eighteenth District from 1945 to 1947.

After losing his reelection campaign in 1946, Doyle won his seat back two years later and served in the House for seven consecutive congressional terms from 1949 until his death in 1963.

Following Doyle's death while in office, President John F. Kennedy offered the following statement about Doyle's career: "During my years of association with him as a Member of the House of Representatives and as President, I respected his dedication to duty and admired his love and compassion for mankind. His death is a great loss to our country and the area he represented so well."

DAVID BURCHAM

As the school grew, it was under steady leadership. Lunt was a capable principal who ended up leaving Long Beach High to become a professor at USC. In 1907, the school hired the man who would shape much of its history. David "Daddy" Burcham became the school's third principal that fall, a title he would hold until 1941, the longest tenure of any principal in school history.

Burcham's hiring in 1907 signaled the end of the school's infancy. To that point, Long Beach High had graduated 165 students in its twelve years of existence, 100 of whom went on to Cal, Stanford or four-year colleges in Southern California. Soon after Burcham took over, the school's enrollment began ballooning, to the extent that the city was quickly looking to build a new school once again.

In the meantime, Poly traditions were popping up all over the place. The girls' basketball team won state championships in 1907, 1908 and 1909, defeating college teams like USC and Cal in the process. The school's track program was founded, as was its music program, which in 1907 included an orchestra, a choir and a mandolin and guitar club.

Students and faculty pose for a photo outside the schoolhouse on the final day of classes at Poly's original campus. *Courtesy* Caerulea *archives.*

In 1909, the Eighth and American campus was bursting at the seams. Originally built with only four classrooms, it was suddenly graduating sixty-five students and trying to find space for tons of new sports teams and music groups.

"I love my athletics, but you love LBHS music," opined one male student to his girlfriend in a yearbook cartoon. There literally wasn't room for all the activities on campus.

Finally, in 1910, the city passed a $240,000 bond to build a new high school at Sixteenth Street and Atlantic Avenue. The name "Polytechnic" was adopted to emphasize that the high school would have both practical courses that could turn out graduates ready for jobs at the docks and college preparatory classes that would prepare other students for four-year universities.

The city already loved its high school, and the bond passed easily. This was in the days when there were no other high schools in town, so everyone rooted for the home team, whether it was in the stands or at the ballot box. Slides were shown in movie theaters promoting Long Beach High baseball games before the movies would start.

The curriculum was rugged, with four years of English, math, Latin and history as well as physics, Greek and other electives thrown in for good measure. The spring of 1911 saw Poly graduate its first one-hundred-student class as the population of the city grew to seventeen thousand. That year also saw the establishment of a municipal water department, the Long Beach Harbor and the municipal wharf.

When school was out for the summer in June 1911, Burcham and his staff locked the doors and left the campus at Eighth and American for the last time, with the knowledge that a brighter future—and a lot more room—awaited them in the fall.

2
NEW CAMPUS, 1911–1932

Classes began at Long Beach Polytechnic High School at Sixteenth and Atlantic on September 9, 1911.

While the school's previous campus was styled after the California missions, Poly's new home was inspired by Roman architecture, and it was grandiose. The school featured grand columns at its entrance and a majestic dome that could be seen for blocks in any direction.

The inside of the campus resembled a university more than a high school. Poly had wisteria arches over its walkways into the quad and large trees for students to sit underneath and study or socialize. A sundial that stood in the corner of the quad helped to tell the time during lunch breaks.

"Our watch word is progress," wrote principal David Burcham.

> *Progress not merely in length and breadth of material expansion, but progress upward toward higher and better things. We trust that the era of unprecedented expansion in facilities and numbers which has been ushered in with the first year in the new Polytechnic school, shall have as its splendid counterpart that truer progress which has character for its ultimate goal, and consists in fostering more and more that training which makes for genuine scholarship, and in surrounding our boys and girls with the influences for stronger, purer, cleaner young manhood and womanhood.*

Burcham was a public education idealist. He genuinely believed in every person's right to free and high-quality schooling. On weekends, after a long week at Poly, he would drive up to the rice fields of North Long Beach and teach the children of Japanese farmers and workers how to read and write English so that they wouldn't be behind on studies when they entered elementary school. At Poly, he made sure that the school's doors were open to all races and backgrounds, and the student body included African American and Japanese students almost immediately.

The year 1911 was a signpost in Poly's history not only because the school moved to its current location but also because the school's sports teams adopted the Jackrabbit mascot. Although it's a unique name, the reason behind it wasn't particularly interesting: the campus was built on an unoccupied field, and there were rabbits everywhere when the doors opened.

At the school's centennial in 1995, the oldest living alumnus at the time was Frank Reagan, class of 1918. He said that the track team in the early 1910s chose the Jackrabbit as its mascot because they were all over the field they trained on.

"And they were swift and strong," he said. "Like us."

It was good that the city had chosen a big lot for its new campus. When the school opened its doors in 1911 there were 850 students attending, with 31 teachers. There were more teachers at Poly in 1911 than there had been citizens of Long Beach just twenty-five years prior when the town decided it needed a school.

COMMISSION GOVERNMENT AND GROWING PAINS

As the campus and student body grew, the Poly student government suddenly found itself running a small city. The student commission was founded and advised by teacher Jane Harnett, who was a central figure as a teacher and administrator at the school until her passing in the influenza epidemic of 1918.

The commission began to face increasing challenges. Because the students had to pay for the cost of the sports teams—they hired and paid the coaches and covered all travel costs—they also had to raise money. That was done in part through the student store on campus, which by 1920 was raking in between $18,000 and $20,000 a year, big money at the time.

It was also done by implementing a fee for students, similar to the ASB fees schools still charge. Poly made history in California by being the first to do that as well, though not without controversy.

The student body on campus posing in front of the school in 1913. *Courtesy* Caerulea *archives.*

In that year's *Caerulea,* "Free education is fast becoming a mere phrase in our modern scholastic world," wrote one indignant student of the $1.50 annual fee.

The commission's elected officers were responsible for the school's assemblies, for all on- and off-campus entertainment and for purchasing items for the school. "The students of Long Beach Polytechnic High School have a privilege not generally accorded to most high schools, in that they have an organized student body with both elective and appointive officers," explains a 1913 yearbook.

The commission organized a trip of several dozen students to Occidental College to see Booker T. Washington speak in 1914 and hired transportation to bring forty students to Los Angeles in 1913 for the first performance of the Los Angeles Symphony Orchestra.

The right to self-govern was not only rare for students of the time, but it also encouraged them to think about social issues. Women wouldn't get the right to vote in America until 1920, but Poly elected its first female student body president in 1917, when Bernice Cole was voted into office.

"Even in high school one can see the results of the feminist movement," reads the 1917 *Caerulea.*

As Long Beach's population continued to grow, Poly's campus transformed from a high school into a round-the-clock education factory. In the 1920s, the student enrollment ballooned to over four thousand students as Poly became the biggest high school west of the Mississippi, a designation it's enjoyed frequently since.

The campus also opened a night school in 1913 to accommodate growing demand for adult education. The night school, which ran six months a year, had 748 students when it began in 1913, offering classes including English for beginners, commercial development, machine shop, sewing, Spanish and woodshop. The school had its own principal (Rexford Newcomb, who went on to teach at the University of Illinois and serve as the dean of fine arts there) and 18 full-time teachers.

It wasn't all studies and political organizing, of course. Poly was quickly overrun with a host of college-style sororities and fraternities. In September 1913, the Scarab Architectural Club was formed, a sorority that still exists on campus today. Comus, Portia, Sphinx and others also began popping up in the 1910s.

JACKRABBIT SPOTLIGHT: HUGO BENIOFF

Hugo Benioff was a 1917 graduate of Long Beach High School who made substantial contributions to the field of seismology and plate tectonics. In 1924, he joined the Seismological Laboratory at the California Institute of Technology, receiving his doctorate from the school in 1935. In 1932, he created a vertical seismometer known as Benioff seismometer—it is currently used in every country in the world.

Benioff would become famous for his work studying earthquake focus depth in the Pacific Ocean. He worked alongside Japanese seismologist Kiyoo Wadati, and together they studied specific zones, named Wadati-Benioff zones, where the ocean crust is subducted, causing deep focus earthquakes down to seven hundred kilometers in depth.

He also made contributions to the creation of musical instruments, including the piano, violin and cello, and spent several years working with the Baldwin Piano Company later in his life. In 1958, Benioff was elected a Fellow of the American Academy of Arts and Sciences.

Among his modern relatives are David Benioff, co-creator of the popular HBO show *Game of Thrones*, and Marc Benioff, the billionaire founder of Salesforce.

SPORTS DOMINANCE

Right from the beginning, Poly enjoyed a huge run of athletic success, something that's been a hallmark of the school for its entire history. The size of the school was certainly a help, as was a population made up of hardworking, blue-collar kids who were often the children of farmers who had moved to Long Beach from the Midwest or of laborers at the city's harbor. In the 1910s, it was common for students to take a year off to work at the docks and then finish school.

Poly is known nationally for football, track and basketball, but the school's first powerhouse dynasty was probably its water polo team. Pete Lenz's water polo squad didn't lose a game from 1916 to 1923, winning seven consecutive California Interscholastic Federation (CIF) championships and producing several Olympians.

"Tradition has it that a Green and Gold football, baseball, or track team may occasionally drop a contest, but should the water polo flotilla be defeated, the result would be disastrous," read the *Caerulea*. "The Long Beach dreadnaughts smoothly sailed on to championship after championship."

Poly was dominant athletically from the start, but the founding of the CIF in 1913 gave the school an official record—between 1913 and 2018, Poly won over 120 CIF championships and 36 state championships, the most of any school in California.

The CIF allowed only boys' sports, meaning that powerhouse programs like the Poly girls' basketball team fell by the wayside, although Miss Vinnie Gee did offer "physical training" classes to girls in 1911, the equivalent of physical education classes, which weren't offered anywhere else for girls in Southern California. In 1915, Poly made physical education a requirement for boys and girls, which California added as a requirement statewide two years later.

The Poly football team was so dominant in the late 1910s that many teams refused to play them. The Jackrabbits of 1919 went undefeated and were crowned CIF, state and national champions, beating Phoenix High 102–0 in a clash of the two top teams in the country. Morley Drury was a star football, basketball and water polo player who went on to great fame at USC.

Students flocked to see the best football team in the country, as twelve thousand were on hand on Poly's campus to see the Jackrabbits beat Phoenix, and another twenty thousand came to see Poly beat down Everett High from Washington the next year.

Long Beach Poly's first CIF championship team, the track team of 1914. *Courtesy Caerulea archives.*

On January 12, 1924, the school dedicated its football field as Burcham Field, in honor of its longtime principal. The JROTC band outlined his initials on the field, and a plaque was dedicated. It remains at the school and reads: "Dedicated by the student body to David Burcham, principal, whose ideals of clean sport and high faith in youth have inspired the indomitable spirit of Long Beach Polytechnic High School."

Poly, meanwhile, kept winning. The boys' swim team won a CIF and national championship in 1932, and Poly students joined a campus Olympic Committee to help gather volunteers for that summer's Olympic Games held in Los Angeles, with rowing events taking place in Long Beach. Poly alum Clyde Doyle was the head of the Long Beach Olympic Committee.

WORLD WAR I

The United States entered World War I in 1917, and the effect was immediately felt on Poly's campus. The school already had an JROTC unit, but its numbers swelled by two hundred on the day that war was declared.

Songs like "Over There" depicted the war as a triumphant effort full of brass and vinegar, but the hundreds of Long Beach Poly grads who were sent to the front quickly learned about the horrors of war.

JACKRABBIT SPOTLIGHT: FRED LAWRENCE WHIPPLE

Fred Lawrence Whipple graduated from Long Beach High School in 1923 and went on to a successful career in astronomy, earning induction into the International Space Hall of Fame in 1984. After leaving Poly, Whipple studied at Occidental College, UCLA and UC Berkeley, where he helped map the orbit of Pluto as a graduate student in 1930, shortly after the planet was discovered. Whipple would go on to discover or co-discover a handful of planets and the asteroid 1252 Celestia.

In 1946, Whipple invented the "meteor bumper" to protect spacecrafts from debris. The thin metal shield was designed to disintegrate space debris like asteroids as it made contact with the craft, and his design, known as the Whipple Shield, is still in use by NASA today. He would make another major contribution to the world of astronomy in 1950 when he theorized about the composition of comets. His "dirty snowball" theory contended that comets were primarily made of ice along with some rock particles as well. Nearly fifty years later, close-up photographs of Halley's Comet in 1986 would confirm Whipple's theory.

Whipple also directed the Smithsonian Astrophysical Observatory (SAO) in Cambridge, Massachusetts, from 1955 to 1973. Under his leadership, that organization was the only one capable of observing and tracking Sputnik, the first satellite put into space by the Soviet Union in 1957. In the years that followed, he helped create the standard techniques for measuring the speed of meteors and computing orbits of comets and asteroids, as well as a theoretical model for describing the structure of comets, which are still used today. In 1963, Whipple received the President's Award for Distinguished Federal Civilian Service from President John F. Kennedy.

Five years later, he set up the Mount Hopkins Observatory in Arizona. The facility is the SAO's largest outside of its home site in Cambridge, and it was renamed the Fred Lawrence Whipple Observatory in 1981. The American Geophysical Union's Planetary Sciences section further honored Whipple in 1989, establishing the Fred Whipple Award, given each year to an individual who makes an outstanding contribution to the field of planetary science.

Students weren't the only ones involved. Poly teacher and football/basketball coach Edgar Kienholtz was called overseas to fight, then returned home to continue coaching, leading the historic 1919 Poly football team.

Poly students did all they could to support their friends and the rest of the American troops. They raised money in 1918 to buy records to send overseas as a Christmas present, they sewed clothes and they came together to purchase $188,353 in war bonds and stamps. The student body also donated clothes and supplies to the Red Cross, adopted thirty-three French and Belgian orphans of the war and sent more than two thousand books to soldiers abroad. "Our school has united to give its all in answer to the need of the hour," read the 1918 *Caerulea*.

After the war ended, graduates of the class of 1919 referred to themselves as the Victory Class, although almost immediately the influenza outbreak would require its own efforts. Mandatory vacations were assigned in October and January, with the *High Life* student newspaper printing classes' assignments for them. On Lincoln's birthday in February, World War I veterans came to speak to students on campus—the blue stars on the service flag at Poly were turned gold to honor the nine alumni who died overseas.

WILSON OPENS, CAMPUS EXPANDS

Poly finally got a local rival in 1926 with the opening of Wilson High on what was then the eastern edge of town. Because there wasn't open enrollment, a somewhat cruel standard was enforced on the town's kids: when Wilson opened, anyone living east of Junipero Avenue had to transfer to the new school.

Two friends could have been living across the street from each other on Junipero and going to school together their whole lives, but if they were seniors in the fall of 1926, one of them would have remained at Poly while the other had to transfer to Wilson. That's not just a hypothetical: it actually happened. Cliff Meyer and Horace Smitheran both lived on the east side of the street and mid-career were moved to Wilson, where they became legendary athletes.

In 1927, the *Caerulea* saluted the Wilson seniors who produced the *Campanile*, the Bruins' yearbook—most of them came from the *Caerulea*'s ranks the year before.

There's no doubt that a new school was needed. When Wilson opened, Poly had more than four thousand students, and the city was growing by leaps and bounds after the discovery of oil in Signal Hill, triggering an oil

The front of the first campus at Sixteenth and Atlantic featuring the school's distinctive dome and arched column entrance. *Courtesy* Caerulea *archives.*

The quad of the first campus at Sixteenth and Atlantic, including the school's beloved wisteria tree. *Photo courtesy LBUSD History book.*

boom and a "black gold rush" later chronicled in Upton Sinclair's novel *Oil!* and its movie adaptation, *There Will Be Blood.* The new campus in town didn't just get a good chunk of Poly's students: George C. Moore, who founded the music programs at Poly, was also transferred to Wilson.

The Poly campus continued to grow, and in 1931 a new auditorium opened at a cost of $200,000, almost as much as the entire campus cost to construct twenty years prior.

Because the Poly students were in charge of the school's finances, the stock market crashes of 1929 and 1932 were felt directly. The commission made a special policy that encouraged saving the revenue from the student store, which at that point was up to $35,000 a year. "The balance from previous years was set in the general reserve fund and in the store equipment reserve fund to be used for permanent improvements or general expense items of a semi-permanent nature," read the new policy.

As the early 1930s marched on, Poly sat secure in its position as a national athletic and academic powerhouse and was taking steps to withstand the Great Depression. Poly students and faculty had no idea how soon a different kind of disaster would strike.

3

THE EARTHQUAKE, 1933

I n the 120-plus-year history of Long Beach Poly, only one day is significant enough to require its own chapter.

The morning of March 10, 1933, began like any other spring day in Long Beach. Students said goodbye to their parents and hurried out the door to school. Boys and girls lingered on the steps up to Poly's front entrance, leaning on the pillars and talking to one another about plans for the weekend.

Poly student Margaret Cuyler penned a remembrance for the *Caerulea* of 1933 of what life was like on campus that day: "The sun's luminous gold paints the eastern side of Poly's dome and slips down to touch the boys and girls thronging the campus as they pass from portico to doorway and out into the patios."

Students moved back and forth from classroom to classroom, stopping for shade under the wisteria arches in the afternoon sun, picking a leaf of ivy off the vines that covered the walls around Poly's quad. With 3,600 students and the nation's best sports program, the activity on campus didn't stop with the end of the school day.

"The hours wane into mid-afternoon," reads the *Caerulea*.

> *The final bell—and from the doors burst laughing crowds of youth, chatting of the good times that are to come with the weekend. There is a water polo game in the swimming pool. The fields are covered with hockey and tennis players and trackmen. The* Caerulea *and* High Life *offices*

hasten to clear up the work for the week, and the L girls gather to banquet in the social hall. Settling down in the later afternoon, Poly's dome is caressed by the rays of a sun that is rapidly slipping away into the coolness of the twilight. One by one the footfalls pass, and only the echoes of friendly voices and happy laughter remain.

At 5:55 p.m., ten minutes of chaos turned the city of Long Beach upside down. A 6.4-magnitude earthquake struck, centered just offshore from downtown Long Beach. The violent shaking rippled up the Newport-Inglewood Fault line, which runs through the city.

Every school in Long Beach collapsed, including Poly.

"Bricks hurtled through the air, great beams are twisted and wrenched as if they were mere sticks, a burning building becomes a huge furnace, and Poly's dome, steeped in tradition and adoration, crashed into a thousand fragments," mourns the *Caerulea*. "Ashes and dust, ashes and dust."

The dome dropped down into the great hall at the front of the campus, destroying everything underneath it. The brick buildings across campus collapsed in on themselves, stairways shattering, chalkboards ripping away from the wall and landing on the desks before them. The beloved wisteria and ivy of the Poly campus were torn apart, and some columns at the school's entrance snapped in half or crumbled into pieces.

Across the city, fifty-two people were killed and more than seven hundred injured. Long Beach's schools were utterly destroyed, as were many of the

The front of the Poly campus, completely destroyed from the 1933 earthquake; Poly's signature dome has collapsed behind the school's arched entrances. *Courtesy Poly historical archives.*

Above: The *Caerulea* room, where Poly's yearbook was produced. The wall has collapsed forward against the school's desks. *Courtesy* Caerulea *archives.*

Left: A view of the Poly quad post-earthquake shows the school's historic sundial, one of the few landmarks to have survived the quake. The base of this sundial still stands in the Poly quad today. *Courtesy* Caerulea *archives.*

city's churches and businesses. In all, $50 million in damage was assessed. Only Poly's auditorium still stood after the shaking and subsequent aftershocks had ceased.

Still, there was a silver lining. Long Beach was a young and family-focused city, and almost a third of the population were school-aged children at the time. The earthquake struck several hours after class had been released. Given that no schools were left standing, it's safe to say that had the earthquake happened six hours earlier there likely would have been tens of thousands of casualties.

One of those near misses was the father of one of Poly and Long Beach's best-known alums. "My dad was across the street from Poly watching all that happen in 1933," remembered Billie Jean King in a recent interview. "It's lucky he was across the street."

As it was, there was only one death on a Long Beach campus, a San Pedro student (Tony Guglermo) who'd participated in a track meet at Wilson High and was still in the shower room there when the P.E. building collapsed.

Charles Francis Seymour, head of Poly's social studies department, said the death count could have been higher at Poly. "Mere minutes before the earthquake the Girls' League and its adviser were hurrying underneath the dome and through the columns to make it home for dinner," he wrote. "A few stragglers rushed from the social hall shortly after the quake began, plaster-covered but uninjured."

Students were given two weeks off of school, while administrators scrambled to assemble a plan for what to do with them. Students and alumni flocked to Poly over the next week to see for themselves what had happened. Guards stood around the campus, keeping employees and students away from the rubble, which was still shifting and remained a major hazard.

"At first, teachers were not even allowed to cross the street," wrote Seymour. "The registrar smiled quizzically and remarked that it was the first time anybody had ever been able to keep him out of his office." A few days later, male teachers were allowed to sign a death waiver to enter the remains of the school, bringing out recovered personal objects for themselves and the female teachers. Students waited in lines outside as teachers filled waste buckets with textbooks and anything they could pry out of busted lockers.

Two months later, on May 17, the school hosted an Alumni Homecoming that was also an Alumni Farewell ceremony, as the city's leaders gathered to say goodbye to the ruins of the campus they knew and loved. More than five thousand alums came to pay tribute before the process of clearing the site began that July.

Two faculty members survey the rubble of what was a classroom building at Poly after the 1933 earthquake. *From Poly historical archives.*

There were several speakers, including Lorne Middough, class of 1912. Middough became a prominent businessman in town, and he was part of the first class to graduate at the campus at Sixteenth and Atlantic. He addressed his fellow alumni and others:

> *In 1911 we moved out into the country to the new Polytechnic High School. That was a banner year. Many victories were won and precedents established. Today, Poly is in ruins. The day after the earthquake with friends I inspected buildings about the city, and I found Poly a total wreck.*
>
> *The dome was down, the trophy room had fallen in, and what hurt me the most was the fact that the pillars of the entrance were badly damaged. My what a story those pillars could tell! Of all the secrets, the excuses for broken dates, the alibis for defeats on the diamond, the gridiron, or the track, those pillars and arches know! Had it not been that other old timers of Poly were there that day, I think my eyes would have filled with tears; but I raised my chin, took a deep breath, and conceived the idea that we alumni of Poly should preserve those arches and pillars.*

Middough led an alumni-organized effort to do just that, raising money and manpower to preserve much of the rubble. Some of the bricks and other masonry went into a time capsule. Four column-tops were preserved

A look down a corridor of the campus shows how devastating the earthquake was and how fortunate the school was that it took place outside of instruction hours. *From Poly historical archives.*

and currently sit on the sides of the campus's flagpole. The sundial was dug out and still sits in the quad today.

The cornerstone of the administration building was also opened and removed by Dr. Henry Booth, the vice president of the board of education. It was Booth himself who laid the cornerstone originally in 1910 when ground was broken on that campus. The 1910 cornerstone also now sits embedded in Poly's flagpole.

There was no doubt that priceless history and tradition were lost, but principal David Burcham was optimistic. "Our buildings are destroyed, but not our school," he told a PTA meeting a few days after the earthquake. "For we have our students and our teachers and the courage to rebuild."

That sense of perseverance and hard-won optimism prevailed among all of the Long Beach administrators.

Walter Hill, president of the board of education, proudly declared, "Although the buildings may be completely razed, Poly's spirit will never die."

Eugene Tincher was a Poly graduate, class of 1908, and a board of education member. He spoke of the opportunity that the city had to use the tragedy as an excuse to create something even better, both at Poly and across the city:

> *The Long Beach of tomorrow will be thoughtful and far-seeing in building its educational system. This will apply not only to buildings and physical equipment, but also to the arrangement of its educational plan. The builders of tomorrow can and should build well because they have at their command the experience of the past.*

4

REBUILDING AND WORLD WAR II, 1933–1945

There's never a good time for an unprecedented natural disaster, but it's worth noting that 1933 was an especially terrible time financially.

The country was in the grips of the Great Depression, with fourteen million unemployed. Still, the city banded together and approved a $4.9 million school reconstruction bond in August of that year, and the federal Public Works Administration agreed to pay 30 percent of reconstruction costs via federal grants, a partnership that also resulted in several historic murals that are still around Poly's campus today. (See chapter 11 for more on the art at Poly.)

With the basic funds secured for reconstructing Long Beach's schools, there were two major challenges for Principal David Burcham and his administration: how to handle the remaining few months of the 1932–33 school year and how to rebuild.

SPRING 1933

Burcham gave his students two and a half weeks off, with class resuming on March 30. The school year was extended by two weeks to the end of June, which left the Poly staff with three months of school left to navigate.

Burcham Field was normally home to Poly's dominant sports teams, but for the remainder of that year and months after, it was home for the entire campus. When students arrived at Sixteenth and Atlantic on March 30, they found stakes in the ground all over the athletic field, with the names of their teachers written on white cards and nailed to them. (See photo insert for an image of the temporary campus arrangement.) Because the auditorium had survived, it was suggested that it host the school, but it was feared that the building would collapse in an aftershock—the same was true of the bleachers around the field.

A bugle call at 9:00 a.m. that morning signaled that school, such as it was, was back in session. Burcham borrowed a broadcasting wagon from Texaco Oil to address the students, a device normally used on Signal Hill to bark instructions from one end of the oil field to the other.

With the rubble of the old campus still surrounding them, students huddled on the grass around their teachers to listen to lectures. Burcham himself would ring a bell into the microphone to signify when it was time to switch classes or take a lunch break. Teachers stood outside in sunglasses and large hats to protect themselves from the heat; those who were beachgoers brought large umbrellas to shade themselves or their students.

When classes began, they were only ten minutes long, but as Burcham worked his city connections, he was able to bring in picnic tables from the city parks, bedsheets, quilts and salvaged blackboards.

"It was a veritable Gypsy encampment," wrote Charles Frances Seymour, the school's social studies department head. "Although it was hot, cold, dry, wet, and windy by turns, with a place to actually sit, school became tolerable and periods lengthened to twenty minutes."

When Howard Hicks became principal two decades later, he said that the images of that spring stayed with him. He wrote:

> I shall never forget the times that I came by Polytechnic High School in the spring of 1933. Its buildings were entirely out of use; their walls were crumbled, and brick lay in confused heaps at the base of various buildings.
>
> In the physical education areas there were stakes with placards tacked to them designating the subject and the teacher where classes met after that historic earthquake. In all the years that have followed, I think I have never seen a time when the spirit of Polytechnic High School was at a higher level than when the students met at fence posts for their classroom stations.
>
> As I looked upon that scene in 1933, I saw the evidence of what we all know to be true: the spirit of institutions resides in people. Loyalties to country, school, and church are the substance of character, ideals and beliefs. They are not destroyed by earthquake or fire; they are the things that America is dedicated to keep alive in the hearts of its people; they are the essence of democracy. The spirit of Polytechnic High School is of that quality.

Burcham laughingly referred to Poly as a new "open air school" but also helped make sure things got back up to speed quickly. The *High Life* newspaper was printing again within six weeks, and the *Caerulea* put out that year's yearbook on schedule. Clubs painted the bricks from the rubble and gave them away to alumni or sold them as souvenirs to raise money for new necessities.

Assisting Burcham was a whole staff of eager teachers and administrators, with an air of excitement about their grand adventure. Registrar Frank Reid had served at Poly with Burcham for decades, and his expertise was necessary. Reid had to record grades, administer the school's finances, handle registration and transcripts and also serve as advisor to the student commission and the yearbook class. With all of his records lost or destroyed, much of that necessary material had to be assembled from scratch in a few short weeks.

Margaret Cuyler wrote a remembrance of attending school in that unique spring:

> *The peal of the bugle sounds, and there is a deep sacredness and thankfulness in the heart of every student as the flag once again journeys heavenward, followed by Poly's green and gold pennant. The whole field is enveloped in silence, and every eye is on the crest of the flagpole.*
>
> *High adventure and a bit of pioneering spirit stride among the young people; and as the classes start, the field is an interesting panorama of groups of students assembled around a teacher. There are still skilled hands but no shops; still busy fingers but no commercial rooms; yet heads buzz with thoughts of line and color.*
>
> *The only semblance of a classroom is a folding chair with a stake to mark the number. The only dome is the caerulean blue of heaven; her walls are the lines of young eucalyptus trees and green fir hedges. Here and there gay red, green, and yellow beach umbrellas add the festive air of a beach party. Flapping tarpaulins are erected as shelters from the sun and wind.*

Students of San Diego High, Poly's big rival at the time, sent seventy dollars to allow the Poly students to purchase a PA system for outdoor assemblies.

The challenges of running a school in those circumstances were many and varied. Recovered library books were stored in the extant corner of the gymnasium. Restrooms had to be constructed on the fly in the gardener's greenhouses with salvaged plumbing fixtures. Because there was only one field for all activity, PE classes and band practice would be going on right next to a math class.

"Everywhere, crowded academic classes competed with the yelling in physical education classes, or the blaring brasses of the ROTC band," wrote Seymour. "It was a character-testing time."

The Armory downtown hosted the school's basketball games, while the concerts were held at the Municipal Auditorium and debates and plays were held at the Masonic Temple.

In that year's *Caerulea*, students penned tributes to Burcham's inspirational leadership style but also reference a surprising side effect of the strange circumstances: the adversity actually brought everyone closer together.

"The school took on an aspect of a jolly beach party with the dignity and seriousness of previous school almost forgotten," wrote student Mary Wright.

> *We came to know our teachers as human beings, a fact we sometimes couldn't realize before. They became our pals, we worked with them. There was real joy in knowing and understanding our teachers, and having them know and understand us. We found that education does not depend upon buildings and equipment but upon mind and spirit. We are coming out of the disaster stronger than we went into it.*

TENT CITY

When the class of 1933 graduated, Burcham and his staff breathed a sigh of relief. Then they immediately got back to work trying to figure out a more tolerable temporary campus situation than beach blankets on the grass. The rubble of the old school was being cleared that summer, which created a little more room.

It was decided that the interim Poly campus would be hosted in tents around Burcham Field until the new campus could be built. In all, seventy-one tents with forty desks each were built on wooden platforms, all of them wired with electricity and gas heating to protect against the cold ocean breeze that had chilled morning sessions. The tents had wood frames with white canvas fashioned to form makeshift walls and beaverboard halfway up on the sides for mounting chalkboards. The tents housed thirty-five to forty students and a teacher, at a construction cost of $250–$325 per tent.

As the campus was being rebuilt, a tent city quickly sprang up on the Poly athletic fields, where students attended classes during construction. *From Poly historical archives.*

Lockers were set up outside, and bricks from the rubble were laid down as walkways between the tents so that students could move from class to class without getting muddy when it rained.

The Poly student commission raised money for small upgrades and helped campaign to pass the school bond; the students also established the Long Beach Poly Chamber of Commerce to try to bring in businesses to partner in the rebuilding effort.

As plans were drawn up for a new campus, Burcham continued to lead Poly's Tent City on the field that had already been named after him. It's a tribute to his influence and skill that the students of the era seemed to actually enjoy going to school in temporary tents.

Burcham's message to his students in the 1934 *Caerulea* provides a good window into his leadership style:

> *Students of Polytechnic—The past two years represent the most interesting period in all our school history. Three thousand students in tent houses, a regular school on full-time schedule with every department functioning efficiently—that, in a word, is the picture.*

Most important of all, in meeting a great emergency a new spirit has been born. The challenge to carry on in the face of physical handicaps and curtailed facilities has developed strength, self-reliance, and resourcefulness, and a happy and democratic atmosphere from our outdoor setting.

Moreover, there is a spirit of optimism, loyalty, and united action that has carried us to unusual triumphs in school activities.

New buildings are rising on the campus. We are beginning to have visions of a magnificent school plant to house the Polytechnic of the future. But we shall be a great school only in the measure in which we carry forward in that spirit which has risen to its greatest heights during the emergency period.

RISING FROM THE RUBBLE

A number of architects worked on the plans for the new school, including Francis Heusel and his partner Kenneth Wing, a Poly alum. The two of them were leading mid-century modern architects in Long Beach who also designed the Long Beach Courthouse and many prominent homes in town. Architect Hugh Davies took inspiration from Heusel and Wing's concepts and made the blueprint, and in 1935 he added a design flourish that would become well known to all Poly students: a copper frame over the main entrance to the school that reads "Enter to Learn, Go Forth to Serve."

Other design elements that were representative of the mid-century modern movement are still found around campus—the art deco copper framings, circular cutouts in walls and for windows. The quad was originally going to be filled with a reflecting pool before school administrators decided they'd rather not have soaking-wet students after every lunch break.

In executing the vision of the school, Davies took into account the complaints of teachers and administrators working in the Tent City: it was too bright outside the tents and too dark inside of them. And, of course, the noise.

"The school will be painstakingly constructed with function, quiet, and light factored in," promised Davies in a yearbook missive as the plans became public.

Students were excited, and as the blueprints and artists' renderings went public, they dreamed of seeing the remaining rubble cleared from around their tent campus and a new school being built in its place.

One of the concept sketches for what would become the "new" Poly in the mid-1930s. *Courtesy* Caerulea *archives.*

An artist's rendering of the plan for Poly's administration building and quad. *Courtesy* Caerulea *archives.*

"In the coming years a new Polytechnic will rise from the ruins of the old," reads the foreword to the 1934 yearbook.

It will be made possible through the vision and foresight of the citizens of Long Beach. This new school will combine the best in architecture with the highest in ideals.

The spirit of the new school will be a combination of the old and the new. It will be one of fresh hope for greater achievement, but it will be inspired by the dignity and strength of past traditions. The architecture and ideals will combine to make a Polytechnic that will carry on the high standards of other years, which will be a realization of the hopes of the present and the vision of the future.

Prominent alum Lorne Middough chaired a Poly High Memorial Committee, responsible for preserving as much of the old campus as possible. The original plan was to have the school's fallen arches reconstructed at one end of Burcham Field so that sports teams entering and leaving the field would pass through them. The plan proved financially and logistically impossible, so instead the committee sold souvenir bricks to pay for a memorial to the old campus, with the 1910 cornerstone and four of the destroyed columns built into the flagpole of the new campus.

Through the mid- to late 1930s, much of the modern Long Beach Poly campus was built.

The administration building went up quickly, followed by the restoration of the auditorium and the 300 and 400 buildings on the front of campus, all of which were finished by the spring of 1936. A few tents remained but weren't used, as more permanent bungalows housed the classes that weren't yet in a real building.

The Poly PTA, the first in the state of California, organized relentlessly to make sure bond money was coming in and to raise funds for other campus improvements, including planting most of the trees that are still in Poly's quad today. As they were planted, each one was dedicated to members of the faculty who'd passed away.

Meanwhile, the city continued to grow and students continued to flock to Poly, as the school's enrollment swelled past 4,000. In 1937, 1,006 students graduated, a record for the school and the state of California.

The school navigated this period of growth smoothly, guided by Burcham, Reid and Evelyn Lofland, Poly's dean of girls. That trio had decades of experience together and used every bit of it to help guide Poly through its

Construction around campus as new buildings went up, with work often done by students after class; retrofitting of the auditorium, the only building to survive the quake. *Courtesy* Caerulea *archives.*

Past, present, and future. Poly Campus

Left: A view of the quad as buildings continued to go up around the open space in 1938. *Courtesy* Caerulea *archives.*

Below: Graduates line up to file into the newly reopened auditorium in 1937. *Courtesy* Caerulea *archives.*

A look up Atlantic at the rebuilt campus in 1938. The outer walls would later be demolished, but otherwise this is the way it's looked for the last eighty years, minus the oil derricks on Signal Hill. *Courtesy* Caerulea *archives.*

recovery. Construction was all over campus, and some students would finish a day of school then clock in for an after-class job working on construction crews, putting up the new PE buildings, the gym or the language arts building.

Poly's sports programs continued to dominate, and a genuine football rivalry with Wilson developed. NFL great Jim Thorpe was one of fourteen thousand fans on hand to watch Poly beat Wilson at an Armistice Day game in 1937. The next year, fan demand forced the game up north to the Rose Bowl, where more than thirty thousand fans took a special trolley from Long Beach to Pasadena to watch a 19–0 Poly win.

By the dawn of the 1940s, the modern campus was basically constructed. Poly graduated 1,250 students in the spring of 1940, students who expressed hope in their senior yearbook that the United States would stay out of World War II. That didn't happen, of course, but before the United States entered the war, Poly High School had to say goodbye to a beloved leader.

BURCHAM RETIRES

The spring of 1941 was the end of an era, with the retirement of David "Daddy" Burcham, who'd been principal of Poly since 1907. Burcham saw Poly through the construction of the first campus at Sixteenth and Atlantic, World War I, the 1933 earthquake and the building of the modern campus. Burcham genuinely loved working at Poly as well as all of the school's students, and he would write hundreds of letters per week to Poly graduates serving overseas in the war.

"They tried to encourage him at one point in his career to go to the Central office to be an administrator and he refused, because it would have meant leaving the kids," said his grandson, David Burcham. "I always thought that was cool. It was really where he wanted to be."

Burcham retired at the dawn of World War II and left students with a hopeful message that reflected his optimistic temperament:

> *In these trying days we find ourselves drawn to a new and increasing appreciation of the priceless heritage that has come down to us as citizens of America. We in the schools will not overlook the fact that the American public school holds a place in our national life which gives it a high rank among the shrines of democracy. From the days of the Little Red School House down to the present time it has been dedicated to the important task of training a loyal and intelligent citizenry, without which democracy cannot long survive.*

The yearbook is filled with tributes to Burcham, including an emotional goodbye from Frank Reid, who served under Burcham for decades as a teacher and administrator.

"His leadership is the type that makes you feel that you are working with him rather than under him," wrote Reid. "The term cooperative which he uses in speaking of our form of student body government applies equally to principal-faculty relationships. His leadership inspires his associates to their best efforts."

Frank Merriam, the governor of California, wrote, "Through the days of sunshine and the hours of adversity and destruction he has remained a never-failing inspiration to his pupils, his fellow teachers and our citizens. Happy is the school, the city, and the state when such men are leaders."

Poly faculty president RE Oliver, on behalf of 120 teachers, wrote, "He is one of Poly's great traditions—he entered Poly to learn, he remained to serve. As he has been our principal in the past, so shall he be our principle in the future."

Deputy Long Beach Schools superintendent Seymour Stone unironically compared Burcham to Abraham Lincoln.

Burcham moved to Long Beach in 1907 to take the job at Long Beach High, and he was so influential that the LBUSD named an elementary school after him. He was also the superintendent of the Sunday school in Long Beach's Japanese church and volunteered with many other organizations. He passed away in 1954 at the age of seventy-nine, but his family has continued to serve the city's schools in the mission of education.

Burcham is buried at Sunnyside Cemetery just a mile and a half from the school he helped mold into a modern powerhouse.

JAPANESE INTERNMENT

Burcham's retirement left Poly without its longtime leader during a time of great crisis. Pearl Harbor was bombed six months after his departure, and America was at war soon after. While the war brought almost indescribable change to every aspect of American life on and off campus, Long Beach and Poly went through some specific challenges as well.

The school had been home to a significant population of Japanese American students for decades. Most of them were the children of either Terminal Island or North Long Beach, where their families worked as farmers and fishermen.

On Terminal Island, south of Poly where the Port of Long Beach is now, a small Japanese town of 3,500 or so residents existed in relative isolation. The children of these farmers, fishermen and cannery workers attended school in Long Beach and San Pedro—many of them attended church in Long Beach and had their earliest schooling from Burcham, who volunteered in that capacity on Sundays.

That entire population was removed from their homes in February 1942 with the signing of Executive Order 9066 by President Franklin Delano Roosevelt. EO 9066 legalized the forced internment of roughly 120,000 people of Japanese descent, most of whom were citizens born and raised in America. Because of Terminal Island's proximity to the Long Beach Naval Base, it was hit fast and hard.

Poly alum Jeanne Wakatsuki Houston spent time on Terminal Island before internment and in the Cabrillo Homes on the Westside of Long Beach after returning from the Manzanar internment camp. Her book *Farewell to Manzanar* is one of the best-known accounts of that era.

She described the scene on Terminal Island in the book: "FBI deputies had been questioning everyone, ransacking houses for anything that could conceivably be used for signaling planes or ships or that indicated loyalty to the Emperor," she wrote. Her father, who was arrested in an FBI raid and sent to a camp apart from his family, burned a Japanese flag and other family heirlooms in the hopes that he wouldn't be seen as an enemy to the country he'd chosen to raise his family in.

"Late in February the navy decided to clear Terminal Island completely," wrote Wakatsuki Houston. "Even though most of us were American-born, it was dangerous having that many Orientals so close to the Long Beach Naval Station, on the opposite end of the island."

Wakatsuki Houston, her family and thousands of others were put on buses and taken to camps.

Terminal Island's residents were the first people of Japanese descent on the West Coast to be forcibly removed from their homes. They were given forty-eight hours to vacate and had to leave behind almost all their possessions, including their furniture, boats and fishing gear.

Three years later, the executive order was rescinded, and families returned home to see that the navy had bulldozed their town. There was nothing left—their boats were gone, their houses destroyed.

Like the Wakatsuki family, many remained in Long Beach, living in the Cabrillo Homes or other low-cost housing. The returning families had to exert pressure to regain ownership of their historic church in downtown Long Beach and their place in the community.

The effect on the Poly campus was eerie. All through the 1930s and early 1940s, there was a Japanese club on campus called the Japanese Friendship Circle club. The students' photo was taken every year on the steps of the auditorium, with membership ranging from a few dozen to upward of fifty students.

Then they disappeared. One day they were on campus, the next, they weren't, with some of them sent to internment camps mere months before they would have graduated. Poly students were sent to Manzanar in California, but also Heart Mountain in Wyoming and Jerome in Arkansas, where seven Poly students ended up according to the camp's high school yearbook, which lists the previous school for its students.

Soon the racist tropes that populated American culture were present on campus, as students held signs with buck-toothed Japanese caricatures on them, bearing slogans like "Bomb de bums wid Bunnie Bombers." It's worth noting that Poly's German Club remained on campus with steady membership during this time.

After the war, Poly's Japanese American population rose again, with most students now living in the Cabrillo Homes according to Wakatsuki Houston; that project was packed with black, Mexican and Japanese families along with poor whites. But even as Japanese American students once again joined the football team and participated in other school activities, there was a new division on campus. Wakatsuki Houston was the first drum majorette of Japanese descent at the school, and she described it as a minor scandal:

> *The band teacher knew I had more experience than anyone else competing that year. He told me so. But he was afraid to use me. He had to go speak to the board about it, and to some of the parents, to see if it was allowable for an Oriental to represent the high school in such a visible way. It had never happened before.*

WORLD WAR II

For the three-thousand-plus students who remained at Poly High for World War II, life changed enormously as well. Howard Hicks was the principal who replaced the legendary Burcham, and his first year saw America enter the war, with many of his students leaving school early or graduating straight into the armed services. Because Long Beach was building ships and planes, every aspect of community life was geared toward the war effort.

The JROTC on campus went from a few dozen students to more than three hundred the day after Pearl Harbor was bombed, and the students formed the Poly Defense Council to help brainstorm ideas for helping national defense. They ended up staging several fundraisers and collecting recyclables.

Smaller sacrifices were made as well. Poly held "Senior Breakfast" instead of prom, with seniors eating a grim-looking meal at the Pacific Coast Club. "As in many activities this change was made due to the war conditions," explained the yearbook.

Plenty of other cutbacks happened on campus. Students went to school with one eye on the war overseas, which many of them knew they'd be joining. At the same time, news came back frequently that former Poly students had been killed in the war.

JACKRABBIT SPOTLIGHT: FRANK EMI

One of the Poly alums who was forced into a camp was Frank Emi, who was sent to Heart Mountain with his wife and children. The Emis owned multiple grocery stores in Long Beach and lost their businesses and livelihood during internment.

Being forcibly removed from their homes and lives to be kept in camps scattered across the country was a great injustice already, but in 1944 the U.S. government also decided that Japanese men were eligible to be drafted into the war effort, even if they were currently in a camp. Emi couldn't stand to see that happen.

"Emi joined six other Heart Mountain internees to oppose the order," said his *LA Times* obituary. "They formed the Fair Play Committee, an ad hoc group that dared to ask how they could be ordered to fight for freedom and democracy abroad when they were denied it at home."

According to the *Times*, the Fair Play Committee was the only organized draft resistance effort in the camps, and over three hundred men ended up imprisoned for refusing to serve. Emi and the other six leaders of the movement were convicted of conspiracy to violate the Selective Service Act. Emi would have received a deferment from service because he had children, but still served eighteen months in a federal penitentiary at Leavenworth before his conviction was overturned in the federal court of appeals.

"We could either tuck our tails between our legs like a beaten dog or stand up like free men and fight for justice," Emi told the *Times* for a feature interview in 1993.

Since the campus was in need of a new building for its library, Hicks suggested it be a Memorial Library dedicated to Poly's fallen soldiers, a dream that became a reality several years later. Hicks originally envisioned the library as a place for statues and plaques for the Poly alums who never came home.

When students turned eighteen, they were frequently sent overseas whether they'd graduated or not, and with many teachers departing campus for the war effort as well, there was a strange air of impermanence on the campus. Social studies teacher and future Poly principal Neil Phillips departed the school temporarily to go to Alaska on active army duty. The curriculum on campus stressed math and science because of their usefulness in the war effort, and PE classes were replaced with military discipline and combat training. Students were buying war savings stamps and bonds to help fund the purchase of fighter planes.

As victory drew nearer, students began to turn their hopes and dreams to the future.

"Winning the war is uppermost in our minds now," read the foreword to the 1944 yearbook. "But we must not forget that after the war will come the peace—after the bombers, the builders. We of this generation will be those builders. Our hands will mold the future: our eyes will see the marvel of things to come."

5

POSTWAR BOOM, 1946–1966

Students fresh back to campus in the fall of 1945 were soon greeted with great news: the United States brought World War II to an end with victory declared on September 2, 1945. The country kicked off a party that seemed to last for fifteen years, and Long Beach was a big part of it. With so much of the war effort tied up in Long Beach, the victory was felt joyously in a town that had built so many of the ships and planes that went to war and sent so many young men.

"This is a year of headlines," wrote Principal Howard Hicks in that year's *Caerulea*. "Historic events compete for our attention. War, peace, revolutions, new governments, and a parade of heroes are in the morning news. Measured by other times, man may now experience a decade in a day."

A CHANGING CITY AND CAMPUS

After World War II ended and the victory parties had died down, the city of Long Beach took a deep breath and took stock of itself. It was a different and quickly changing place. Because of the jobs in airplane and ship construction as well as in the oil fields, more than 170,000 workers had migrated to the city.

Those workers brought families—and students for Long Beach Poly and the rest of the Long Beach schools.

Poly already had a diverse student population, with black, Japanese and Hispanic students attending the school dating back to the 1920s. Walter Ray McCowan, an African American student, was the football team's quarterback in 1932, something that would have been unimaginable across much of the country even decades later.

But while Poly had always been somewhat diverse racially and socioeconomically, the school had been predominantly white for its history. Bill Barnes, class of 1948, said that he was the only African American student on the basketball team when he attended Poly: "There were maybe fifteen black students at the time," said Barnes in a recent interview. "There weren't all the special programs there are now—I was in college prep and I didn't have any classes with any black students because they weren't in college prep."

That quickly changed throughout the late 1950s as more and more families moved to the city in search of work. Affordable housing sprang up on the Westside, which became home to many minority families. Barnes's family was from Los Angeles but moved to the Cabrillo homes in 1945 when his father got a job in the shipyard. He points out that even though the population of African Americans was growing in Long Beach, it wasn't a monolithic group.

White and black students at Poly had different off-campus hangouts in the 1950s and '60s, but this integrated sophomore dance in 1955 shows that the school was ahead of much of the country, too. *Courtesy* Caerulea *archives.*

Poly returned to prominence on the gridiron in the 1950s; here, star athlete and future Long Beach city councilman Dee Andrews runs through a tackle in 1958. *Courtesy* Caerulea *archives.*

"We had to get used to all the guys coming from the South, they were coming from a place where the schools were not integrated, the black students from the South had never gone to school with white students before," said Barnes.

"Most of us came from the South," said Poly All-American football player and track star Dee Andrews, who graduated in the late 1950s and who is now Long Beach's vice mayor. "There were a lot of different kinds of people at Poly, but we had not a moment of racism, we melted in with each other like a family."

Andrews said black students had to be wary of visiting white friends' houses in affluent Bixby Knolls and to stay away from other neighborhoods, but that the atmosphere on campus was friendly.

"Well, we all grew up on campus," said Don Norford, class of 1964, and arguably the school's greatest coach.

Everyone in the neighborhood, we played on campus all the time—we had a roller derby in the quad, on Tuesday nights we'd be in the gym for dances, playing hide and seek with the girls. That gave us all a closer connection to the school and each other, and we looked up to the athletes like Dee and Willie Brown. You weren't a man if you didn't go to Poly.

THE GOLDEN ERA

The late 1940s through the mid-1960s are an undeniable golden age in Long Beach Poly history. The Jackrabbits rode a growing city and increasing diversity to an unprecedented run of athletic dominance, winning a string of basketball, football and track CIF championships. World-famous alums like Billie Jean King and Martha Watson attended the school, though they weren't allowed to compete on real sports teams, because none existed on the girls' side.

Off the field, construction continued to boom. Poly built a Memorial Library, a shop building, a gymnasium and a natatorium, all designed by campus architect Hugh Davies. The school modernized Burcham Field and put up permanent bleachers, as well as an JROTC building and a rifle range. The music program got its home in a new building attached to the back of the auditorium. Students often worked part-time jobs on the construction crews that were expanding their campus.

Jackrabbit Spotlight: Don Norford

Norford grew up climbing over a wall on the back side of Poly with his friends from Roosevelt Elementary, sitting under the shade of a mulberry bush to watch track meets and dream of one day being as fast as Dee Andrews. He did end up running track and playing football in the early 1960s, but where he made his mark was coming back to serve as a campus security officer and coach with the school's track and football teams from 1976 until his retirement in 2014. In those thirty-eight years, he coached forty-five future NFL players on Poly's football team and became the only assistant coach to ever be named NFL High School Coach of the Year in 1996.

The track is where Norford's influence was felt most deeply after being hired as head coach of Poly's boys' and girls' teams in 1989. Norford's Poly teams won eighteen state titles and twenty-five CIF Southern Section championships. To put those numbers in perspective, Norford retired with more state championships in his sport than had been won by any other high school in the state across all sports.

Among his many anecdotal accomplishments are convincing Willie McGinest to play football as well as basketball. Norford's athletes at Poly won 61 state championships in individual events and 150 CIF-SS individual golds. He coached several athletes who went on to become Olympians, including Bryshon Nellum and Ariana Washington.

"We didn't do anything that other people weren't doing," he said. "We worked hard, we believed in the kids and we loved the kids. We were blessed with some tremendous athletes."

Norford and his wife, Carol, were Poly institutions, welcoming kids into their home when they needed a place to stay and serving as a second set of parents for generations of Long Beach kids. Norford has remained humble even as he's won a ton of awards, including recently being a member of the first class inducted into the National High School Track & Field Hall of Fame.

"When Carol and I were at the NFL banquet, we were sitting down and they got gold everything: gold plate, gold everything," said Norford. "And we looked at each other and laughed like, 'Oh wow, we royalty. We were having a lot of fun with it.'"

Memorial
Library

Poly's newly opened Memorial Library in 1953; the library was dedicated to the Poly alums
who passed away while at war. *Courtesy* Caerulea *archives*.

In 1954, twenty years after the post-earthquake rebuilding began,
Principal Odie Wright declared the campus done. "In the coming year we
will see the completion of the grounds and most of the buildings planned for
our campus," wrote Wright. "A beautiful high school made possible for all of
us through the vision and generosity of the citizens of Long Beach. Today,
twenty years later, we are seeing a completed Poly High School campus."

The size of the school's enrollment grew, too, to well over four thousand.
The Long Beach School District opened new high schools in East Long
Beach (Millikan High) and Lakewood to try to deal with the population
boom and the growing suburbs on the eastern edge of the city. While Poly

remained a relatively harmonious place, that new housing development led the city itself to growing racial isolation, with minorities living downtown, around Poly and on the Westside and white families living in Bixby Knolls, along the shore and in the suburbs to the east.

On campus, the enrollment in the JROTC dropped from hundreds to a few dozen, as students turned their focus from war to fun. Fraternities and sororities were the hot thing once again at Poly, as hundreds of students joined up with Scarabs or Comus, organizing and attending parties. The school's Christmas concerts became enormous productions celebrating the American way of life.

"We were all rooting for each other in all our different sports and activities," remembers Billie Jean King.

The Japanese community reintegrated into Poly, and the students quickly won over acceptance. Toot Uchida and Ray Sugiyama were both elected student body president during the mid-1950s, and in 1957 the school hosted its first International Carnival, an event that still lives on today as the Poly Intercultural Fair.

"The feeling of bringing the world closer together is not a new idea here at Poly, for Poly has been for many years a cosmopolitan student body," wrote student Matty Sloan at the time, exhibiting both Poly's diversity and the student body's pride in that fact.

In the late '50s, more construction began, as Poly put in its signature rose bushes in the quad in 1959, donated by the class of '52—when viewed from above, the benches and planters show "52" as their design. A new cafeteria was built along with a new classroom building and covered walkways.

Off campus, students cut loose at the Hutch, a dance hall that was run for and by students, with annual memberships that gave students access to ping-pong and pool tables, televisions, jukeboxes and other fun. In keeping with Poly students' air of self-determination, officers were elected by the student body to run the Hutch.

As Andrews and other students from the time often bring up, the campus's racial harmony often disappeared immediately after Poly kids walked off campus. That was true of the socializing as well. While white students frequented the Hutch, black students had their own off-campus hangout, the Teen Tavern.

"While there were no implicit rules that stated who had to go where, the segregation was well understood," wrote Poly alum Bob Bro in a blog post.

"Poly during this time was like a college," said Gene Washington, a football star at Poly and the school's first black student body president. "There were

JACKRABBIT SPOTLIGHT: GENE WASHINGTON

Washington was elected Poly's first African American student body president in 1964–65.

"Bill Mulligan, our basketball coach, he really encouraged me to get involved in the student government and run for president," said Washington. "It was kind of unheard of at that time. There was a lot going on around the country and in California, but my coaches and teachers wanted me to get involved—there weren't any issues with it."

While racial division would rip the campus apart in the coming years, Washington said Poly in 1965 was a peaceful place. "We never felt, or I never felt uninvited," he said. "Poly was very far ahead of the rest of the country, no question about it. We never felt like there were any major issues when I was there."

Washington went on to an outstanding football and academic career at Stanford and in the NFL, eventually rising to the level of the NFL's director of football operations. He was the embodiment of the school's new motto, coined in the 1950s by principal Neil Phillips: the Home of Scholars and Champions.

In his acceptance speech upon his history-making election at Poly, Washington said, "During my three years here at Poly, I have been fortunate enough to have participated scholastically and athletically in Poly High life and gained an insight into the concentration and hard work necessary for success. In each area Poly stands on the highest pedestal obtainable."

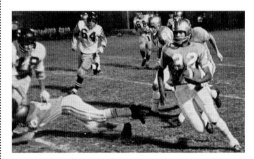

Gene Washington would go on to a stellar career in the NFL as a player and executive. At Poly, he was a unifying figure as both a football star and the student body president. Here, Washington carries the ball in 1963. *Courtesy* Caerulea *archives.*

fraternities and sororities, and they'd been there a long time. The kids were in the same ones as their parents where when they were there—those were white organizations at that time, and they ran everything at the school. There weren't black kids in those clubs. Some of my best friends were in those social clubs—they weren't racists or anything like that, but that's the way it was at the time."

Things on campus were going great. The football team boasted stars like Washington, Earl McCullouch and Marvin Motley in the early 1960s. Martha Watson set a new national record for women in the long jump while still a student, and Billie Jean King started her record-breaking tennis career. Poly's baseball team won a CIF championship in 1963, with Willie Brown and Oscar Brown starring in multiple sports in addition to their success the diamond. Famous alums came back to the school as Watson made the Olympics in 1964 and returned with her hardware, and John Rambo brought back his Olympic bronze medal.

Poly was the national model for integrated education in the classroom and on the playing field. When Washington graduated and headed to Stanford, he was aware that there had been racial unrest at other Southern California schools—but he said he couldn't imagine it happening at Poly.

6

RACE RIOTS AT POLY, 1967–1972

While many students from the 1950s and 1960s have sunny memories of their time at Poly, there were divisions on the campus that were beginning to grow deeper, divisions that would ultimately fracture the campus in three major upheavals: a protest and walk-out in 1967 and campus-wide race riots in 1969 and 1972, as well as several skirmishes in between.

The rest of campus life continued to hum along: the school won several CIF championships in different sports, and the Neil Phillips Hall of Fame opened in 1967, housing many of the school's trophies and awards, as well as the official Poly seal.

The Native Sons of the Golden West paid for a plaque at Eighth Street and Long Beach Boulevard, commemorating Poly's first location. (The plaque is still there today.) The school celebrated its history even while dealing with a troubled present. Billie Jean King came back to speak, and there were a ton of festivities surrounding the school's seventy-fifth anniversary in 1970, which included a small earthquake that was a reminder of the 1933 disaster.

The school was going through its own kind of upheavals at the time. Poly added staff members like Al Nichols and Lonzo Irvin, both great former Poly athletes, to serve as community liaison officers, trying to bridge the gap between a mostly white administration and an increasingly African American community. Despite that fact, at one point in the late 1960s, ten of the eleven counselors on campus were white, along with the entire senior administration.

The Black Students' Club is a worthwhile organization which enables students to understand and to become acquainted with the past and contemporary black culture.

In order for the club members to get new and different ideas, discussion groups and debates which tend to reveal varied points of view are a major part of the club's activities.

Black Students' Club

Brotherhood of Races

The Brotherhood of Races stands for what its name implies. Getting students together on Poly's campus through community service, social activities, and campus improvement projects has been the efficacious goal of this new club. Through their personal associations with each other, the members are building their own feelings of brotherhood and hope that their service activities are building good will and aiding understanding among non-members. As long as there are idealistic, dynamic students and a need for extended understanding, there will be a need for the Brotherhood of Races.

As racial tensions on campus and in the surrounding community increased in the late 1960s, on-campus clubs like the Black Students' Club and the Brotherhood of Races sought to advocate their positions. *Courtesy* Caerulea *archives.*

Poly students began to organize, as the Black History and Culture Club was formed and grew quickly, along with the Mexican-American Students club. Those who were hoping for an escape from the increasingly complex world that included rising racial tensions on campus and the military draft into the Vietnam War formed other clubs, like the Long Beach Local Smials, a club dedicated to *The Lord of the Rings* and the works of J.R.R. Tolkien.

In 1968, Mercedes Mynatt was the first black student to be voted Homecoming queen—despite a growing African American population on campus over the previous two decades, Mynatt was the first African American to even be a finalist for the honor. Another black student, Gail Elder, was voted Homecoming queen in 1970. The next year, the student body would vote to end the Homecoming court tradition, as racially aligned voting had made it into too controversial a topic.

APRIL 1967

Poly and the nation were in a state of agitation and rapid change moving into the late 1960s, with protests raging about the Vietnam War. Southern California was rocked by the Watts Riots in 1965, with six days of violence in Watts and Compton spurring white flight not just there but throughout the region.

On April 11 at Poly, two students got into a fistfight. The two knew each other well, having both played in the same band off campus. One was white; one was black. An argument between the two of them in a morning physical education class spilled over into a hallway fight, with punches thrown.

James Steveson, Poly's then head of the PE department and a swimming and water polo coach, broke up the fight.

So far, the events described could have been written about a thousand different days in the history of Poly—a small fight, quickly broken up with no serious injury. But, as longtime Long Beach football coach and historian Dave Radford pointed out, this was the start of a half decade of open tumult at a school that had once been the pre–*Brown v. Board* model of integrated education.

"We are still living in the lights and shadows of that month," said Radford, who was a third-year history teacher at Poly that year.

The unrest began because it was perceived that Steveson, a white teacher, took the side of the white student in breaking up the fight, handling the black student too roughly.

"The Negro kept trying to hit the Caucasian," Steveson told the *Press-Telegram*. "The Negro was outraged. He was completely out of control. I was trying to prevent him from injuring himself or the other boy and getting in real trouble."

The black community didn't buy the explanation, and the *Press-Telegram* reported that seven adult leaders in the community spoke with Poly principal Walt Newland the next morning, accusing Steveson of "brutality" and "unnecessary force" in the newspaper.

Newland and the school district led a cursory investigation of the incident and quickly backed the teacher's account. "There is no doubt that Mr. Steveson acted prudently in breaking up a fight last week at Polytechnic High School," said a statement from the LBUSD superintendent's office. "The investigation also brought out that Mr. Steveson probably prevented a much more serious problem by his prompt and firm action."

If the school and district administration thought that a quick statement was going to be the end of the matter, they had the wrong community and the wrong time. Poly students organized, with all fifty-one black athletes on Leon Foreman's nationally ranked track program walking out in solidarity on the day of a huge league meet against Wilson. Foreman dismissed those players from the team, further inflaming community anger.

The Long Beach NAACP got involved quickly, with several prominent community members and Poly alums also standing in support of the black Poly students.

Long Beach NAACP president Dr. Fillmore Freeman acknowledged that the issues happening on campus were connected with the larger unrest of America. "Long Beach is part of the nation, and Poly is a part of Long Beach," Freeman told the *Press-Telegram*.

Parents of the suspended track athletes threatened to picket the school if their kids weren't reinstated and met with the board of education several times.

"That is our minimum demand," Clyde Taylor of the NAACP told the *Press-Telegram*. "I think we should limit ourselves to this right now, but we should not lose sight of our other complaints about Poly. This incident is just a symptom of the sickness of the school."

The communication gap between white and black students was apparent in the *High Life*, Poly's student newspaper, which had no mention of the walkout by the track stars, only bemoaning a lack of depth on the team leading to losses to Wilson and Lakewood.

Community leaders like Richard Harris, director of the Neighborhood Adult Participation Project, and Ernest Clark Jr. of the Project Head Start were in constant communication with Odie Wright, LBUSD superintendent (and a Poly alum), as well as Newland.

The community's issues with the school, including the nearly all-white makeup of its administration, became a flashpoint for protest and conversation around its issues with the city as a whole, a city that was becoming increasingly racially segregated. At a news conference at Cal-Rec Center across the street from Poly, community groups asked the Long Beach Police Department to de-escalate the situation in the neighborhood by decreasing its presence and only staffing officers with at least five years' experience.

They also asked for help at Poly and demanded the formation of an interracial human relations commission to investigate conditions on campus, which the LBUSD board granted funding for. The stress of all this wore on the school, both the student body and the administration—Newland literally had a heart attack after one school board meeting and was hospitalized for a week.

The issues spread off campus, and five Poly-area students (all of whom attended Reid High in Long Beach) were arrested after a fight with police near campus. Firebombs were thrown into supermarkets in the area that evening.

That conflict underlined the strife between the community and the police that the African American leaders of the city were hoping to alleviate. In a separate incident, five black teenagers had been hanging out at a marketplace a few blocks from Poly and two gum machines that were standing against the market's open door were bumped and broke.

Because they fell against the door, they set off a silent alarm that brought police. Because it was a silent alarm, police assumed there was a robbery in progress and raced up to the market with guns drawn. It's understandable that the police would have approached with caution, and it's also understandable that the community would want the same de-escalated response that would likely have been drawn by a silent alarm in the Long Beach suburbs. It was the kind of friction that the city was dealing with all over in the late 1960s and early 1970s.

If there was a bright spot to the first round of clashes between the community and the school administration, it was the formation of the Interracial Human Relations Commission, headed by 1948 Poly alum Bill Barnes; that effort would evolve into the group that would save the school a decade later.

MAY 1969

Poly brought in a new principal, Genero Garcia, to help right the ship. Garcia was principal at Stephens Junior High on the Westside and was thought of as a receptive mediator between the establishment and the community. He heard the recommendations of the Human Relations Commission and began implementing many of its requests, especially the desire to see more black representation in the school's staff.

In 1968, he told the *Press-Telegram*, "Where the school had eight Negroes employed in non-teaching jobs last year, there are now 20. There were no Negroes in advisory positions in 1967, today we have 13."

He also said he welcomed the input of the committee. "We find the committee provides rapport between the community and the school," he said.

However, the way forward was neither smooth nor clear.

On May 27, 1969, a "violently anti-Negro bulletin" of "Neo-Nazi type propaganda" was printed and distributed around campus, according to the *Press-Telegram*. The inflammatory bulletin referred to black students as inhuman and frequently used racial slurs.

"They were dropped onto campus by a Neo-Nazi group," said Don Wallace, a student at the time whose mother was on the school board. "Some of my friends and I, black friends and white friends, were running around trying to pick them up before anyone else saw them because we knew what would happen."

That afternoon, there was widespread fighting with more than one hundred students involved, twenty-three of whom were hospitalized.

Two days later, 100 police officers, many wearing riot gear, gathered in front of the school to separate 200–300 "loud but otherwise orderly" white students and parents and 150 black students who marched to the school from King Park, according to the *Press-Telegram*. The police successfully kept the groups apart, but the community was furious and wanted answers about who had printed and distributed the bulletins threatening their children.

The campus closed for the rest of the week, and teachers and administration spent that time and the three-day Memorial Day weekend brainstorming, while black parents called for Garcia's resignation.

School reopened on Tuesday with police searching all students entering for weapons or racist literature, and the Long Beach Unified School District launching a phone line dedicated to listening to "rumors" about the incident. The phone line didn't turn up any info but did receive several panicked phone calls from white parents saying they'd heard the Black Panthers were going to show up with guns and from black parents saying they'd heard the Hells Angels would show up with guns.

A police investigation ultimately ruled that the bulletins had indeed been printed off-campus by an organized hate group (they bore the insignia of a South Bay Neo-Nazi outfit) and distributed by a student or an interloper who snuck on campus. That the message was brought in from off-campus didn't matter. The bulletins exposed the deepening racial divide at the school.

APRIL 1972

The school continued to implement the changes requested by the neighborhood community, hiring more black staff, painting buildings and planting more trees and foliage to make the campus look more inviting. Garcia departed the school and was replaced by Principal Jack DuBois, who was hopeful he could help chart a way forward.

"Nowhere else is it possible to see the traditions and heritage of a glorious past combining with the challenging needs of the present," he wrote in an introduction to the school's students. "Poly, with its multi-ethnic student body, enhanced by a rich and varied cultural heritage, provides a living laboratory for its students and presents them with life experiences that students at other schools are forced to read about or view from a distance via television or the movie screen."

The events of April 1972 did indeed play out like a movie, as the rising racial tensions at Poly and in Long Beach reached a boiling point.

On Sunday, April 23, there was a violent incident at the Rivoli Theater in downtown Long Beach. Newspapers reported that eight black juveniles were arrested after a fight in the theater spilled out onto the street. The windows of the movie theater box office were smashed, along with the concession stands and windows of nearby businesses—several were injured by hurled objects, including a seventy-five-year-old passerby on the street.

According to newspapers, the cause of the fight was either an usher trying to convince a theatergoer to quiet down or asking them to put out a cigarette. One thing was clear: the usher was a white Poly student and the theatergoer was black. When a plainclothes police officer in the theater got involved in the dispute, things quickly spun out of control.

According to Bill Barnes, a Poly grad and the head of the Human Relations Commission, the stories were a fiction easily eaten up by the city's reporters. From the perspective of the black community, it was a racially motivated attack, with the white usher and police officer abusing a black student in the crowd and then starting a fight with her friends when they rushed to her defense.

"I wasn't there, but I had close friends there," he said. "The white students didn't want black students included at that theater. We had theaters on the Westside and by Poly we were supposed to go to. There was a skirmish, and since black kids didn't usually go to that theater, there weren't many of them—so they got beat up."

The next day was Monday at Poly, and it started out like any other day and any other week. But students knew something was going to happen. Carl Cohn, a native of the Poly neighborhood who was then serving as a counselor at the school, heard buzz about it: "A student of mine walked into the career counseling center that morning and said, 'You know there's going to be trouble here today.' And I said, 'Noooo. This is Poly. I know stuff happened in the past, but we've got this.' A couple of hours later, there's 500 kids fighting in the quad."

According to a police report cited in the *Press-Telegram*, eight to ten black non-students from the community scaled a fence at the back of campus, looking for revenge against the white usher from the Rivoli Theater. There was so much underlying resentment and anger that almost immediately, white and black students were squaring off against one another whether they were a part of the original incident or not.

Future Olympian John Rambo, a black student, along with his friend Ron Beaulac, a white student, stood at the doors to the 100 building and watched the chaos unfold, speechless. The fighting spread and spread until anyone in the quad got pulled into it, with trash cans being thrown down from the catwalks onto students below.

"There was so much anger that it exploded really quickly," remembered Shawn Ashley, a senior at the school that year and a future principal at Poly. "After lunch, a fight would break out in a hallway and then another fight would break out, it just kept happening throughout the entire afternoon."

Ashley tried to break up a fight and got sucker-punched by a non-student. Cohn remembered that the fighting was so bad and so widespread that after hours of breaking up interracial fights, some members of the administration were about ready to give up, and when a fight broke out between black students they didn't want to intervene.

"Some people were like, 'Well, it's two black kids…' and I was like, 'Come on folks, come on. We've got to break this up,'" he said.

Teachers opened their classrooms to let in students who were trying to avoid the fracas, and they ended up huddling in there for the rest of the afternoon.

Police officers were summoned to the school but remained outside of the campus as the administration tried to quell the violence, fearing that if police entered it would escalate the situation. According to the *Press-Telegram*, one student was hospitalized and another twenty-eight treated on-site for their injuries, with twenty-one students suspended from school.

Tuesday and Wednesday saw very few students on campus, with a heavy police presence intended to help families feel safe. It was, obviously, too late for that. Ashley was back that next morning, with eight stitches in his mouth.

"For me it was one of those, 'You're not going to scare me off' things," he said. "But it was a ghost town. I'd go into class and there'd be five kids in there. African American families kept their kids home, white families kept their kids home. Everyone was worried. And there had to have been twenty police officers on campus."

Many students didn't return until the following week, and an uneasy peace settled over the campus as two police officers remained on site the rest of the school year. Ashley said that some students were pulled into the racial strife, while others weren't.

"It was never an issue for me. I had a lot of good friends at the school and it was an outsider who hit me, so it just felt like a random thing," he said. "But a lot of people got into this black versus white thing."

Connie Loggins, Poly class of '74, recalls a similar feeling at the time from a black student's perspective; that the problems were generated by external forces, and the Poly community was cohesive enough to overcome the challenges it faced.

"It was definitely disturbing because I did see it erupt on campus," recalled Loggins, who went on to be one of the top administrators at the school.

I will say when I was at Poly it was an outsider that came onto our campus that started it, and that's what fueled it, and then everybody jumps in and then there's this tension and division for a while.

We really were friends, but you're really apprehensive about where that person stands. What do they really think about me? Where are their heads at? But we took our signal from the head. There had to be signals that we were all one Poly, and we came back together. That [disturbance] couldn't continue to fuel itself, there was no life given to it after those perpetrators were dealt with and suspensions were in place. When people came back, we

Poly student Shawn Ashley raises his hand in class. Ashley would go on to return to Poly and become the second-longest tenured principal in school history, overseeing a new golden age. *Courtesy* Caerulea *archives.*

said "Okay, bury the hatchet and move forward." We're kids, we're very impressionable, but the tone was set that we're family. And to this day we still are family.

A CROSSROADS

It was a perilous time for the school, a crossroads not between excellence and mediocrity but between existence and nonexistence. Long Beach Poly had stood for more than seventy-five years at the center of the Long Beach community, known across the country for athletic and academic prowess. For much of that time, it was also a shining example of racial harmony, a school that was voluntarily and successfully integrated.

Now, deep divisions threatened Poly, as they threatened so many other schools in Southern California. In his book *One Great Game*, Don Wallace wrote about the dire situation:

> *"White Flight" became a theme in Long Beach, and the question of who would go to Poly, the only high school out of five with a black and minority population, obsessed everyone from the old elite to the anxious white lower class to the vulnerable and put-upon black community. By 1969 the school was in the heart of a ghetto; violent riots in 1969 and 1972 shattered the campus. Federal authorities who arrived in the aftermath of the riots publicly weighed taking over Poly—and the Long Beach Unified School District. A proud city was left reeling.... [T]he original high school of Long Beach had become a national symbol of democratic dystopia.*

The city, the school board and Poly's administration wondered what to do. They would all play their part in the coming decade, but it was a dedicated group of parents, alumni, students and community members who would make all the difference. The Poly Community Interracial Committee (PCIC) stepped up to the plate, a gathering of black and white members of the city determined to forge a new future for Poly.

"The fights happened on Monday and we met the next week," said Barnes, the first chairman of the PCIC. "People got it. They realized we had to fix this right now."

7

BACK FROM THE BRINK, 1972–1985

There are too many awards to count in the Phillips Hall of Fame at Long Beach Poly. CIF and State championships, displays about the school's athletic dominance and signed memorabilia from all-star athletes like Tony Gwynn and Willie McGinest fill the glass trophy cases that line the hallway between the 300 and 400 buildings.

Behind one of those trophy cases, tucked under a table in a small crawlspace, is a nondescript white storage box, weathered from four decades of age. The box contains the official records of the Poly Community Interracial Committee, and it tells a story unique in American education.

Carl Cohn rose from the ranks of a first-year counselor at Poly during the 1972 riot to become a nationally lauded superintendent of the Long Beach Unified School District. He's since served at the highest levels of the state's public education system and is considered a national expert in the field.

"Of the schools across the country that experienced riots in the late '60s and early '70s, if you go to those schools today, they are pretty much either out of existence or one-race minority schools," said Cohn. "The Poly story is a remarkable story, and basically, in my judgment, the credit goes to the PCIC and the school board."

THE PCIC

The PCIC was known by many names in Long Beach. It was originally formed under Barnes's stewardship following the 1967 incident, after the LBUSD board approved it as an independent entity operating separately from the school, the district and board administrations. Referred to as the Human Rights Commission, the Concerned Poly Parents Group and other less formal names, the PCIC originally represented primarily the concerns of the black community around Poly.

In the wake of the initial unrest at the school, the group successfully advocated for the hiring of more black staff on the campus and cosmetic changes to Poly that made it look more like the suburban school it was at its inception. Because of Poly's prominence in the community, this volunteer group was covered extensively in the press, with front-page newspaper updates on its progress.

Two years after the violence in '69, the PCIC was considered a success, and it very publicly began to transition its purpose.

"The Poly Community Interracial Committee has shifted focus from crash programs in times of crisis to long-term solutions to prevent crises," began a front-page article in the *Press-Telegram*.

Barnes is quoted in the article saying that the problems that had caused Poly's unrest were far from solved, but that it was obvious the board of education saw a different role for the PCIC. Barnes said the PCIC planned on continuing to advocate for more minority staff at Poly, and to follow up on any allegations of mistreatment by Poly students.

That article ran less than a month before the '72 riots—after the violence, the PCIC had to reenter crisis mode, and fast.

The group was made up of representatives from different interested groups. Representing the black community were prominent parents and alumni, including Barnes, Mary Butler, Dorothy Price and Dale Clinton. Poly's white families were represented by Nancy Latimer and Rosemary Ashley (Shawn Ashley's mother), among others. Elizabeth Wallace was a Poly alum, a Poly mom and a member of the school board, and she represented the board at many PCIC meetings, while Cohn and Principal Jack DuBois represented the school's administration. Poly students also served on the PCIC to bring a direct voice from the campus.

By coincidence, Barnes and Latimer were both Poly graduates from the class of 1948, the same class that also produced Long Beach's only three-term mayor, Beverly O'Neill. By an even greater coincidence, one

The students on the Poly Community Interracial Committee in 1976. *Courtesy* Caerulea *archives.*

that makes the PCIC drama almost seem like a movie script, the school's attendance counselor and a PCIC member at the time was David Burcham, the grandson of the school's longtime principal.

Burcham would go on to become the first lay president of Loyola Marymount University, but at that time he was a young up-and-comer along with Cohn.

"We raised a little hell in our day, challenging some decisions that had been made at the district level," Burcham remembered recently with a chuckle. "The PCIC were really pioneers in trying to figure out how to make integrated education work in a way that was fair to everyone."

The meetings took place frequently, all over town. The Latimers and Wallaces hosted in the more affluent Bixby Knolls neighborhood north of the school, while Butler and Price hosted the group in their homes closer to the Poly campus. The PCIC also held many meetings in Poly's faculty lounge over the years, as well as local churches.

"They were coming over three, four times a week for months," remembered Don Wallace, Liz's son, a Poly student who was often invited to sit in on meetings unless it looked like a particularly contentious debate might erupt. "She had a high sign she'd give me when it was time for me to scram."

ENDLESS MEETINGS

When Cohn, Ashley and other education experts are asked what set Poly apart from other schools that experienced racial violence, the consensus was that the PCIC made the difference. But the reason that the PCIC members give is that Poly, unlike many other schools, had all aspects of the Long Beach community maintaining a vested interest in its success.

Cities like Compton and Los Angeles experienced transformational white flight. Poly's attendance district in Long Beach encompassed the wealthier and historic Bixby Knolls neighborhood, as well as the more urban area around the school. Both of those communities, as well as the school board and city government, wanted to see the school survive.

That was the driving factor behind a diverse group coming together for endless meetings, held all over town. Asked how often the PCIC was meeting after the '72 riot, Barnes laughed. "We met all the time," he said. "Once a week, twice a week, three times a week, for years."

These meetings were not the stuff of Hollywood scripts. It wasn't a happy-go-lucky group of can-do adults dedicated to a common cause; it was a diverse coalition with sometimes differing agendas. Nancy Latimer and her husband, Bill, knew that there was a problem when two white families moved out of the tight-knit Bixby Knolls community specifically so that their soon-to-be high school–aged children wouldn't go to Poly.

"When white flight started here with two families moving, we got really strong on getting people to start talking about it," remembered Nancy in a recent interview. Latimer's father graduated from Poly in 1920 and she graduated in 1948, and they didn't want to see the family's ancestral school pushed to the side.

"It was really important to me to keep Poly going, it's in my blood," she said.

> *I think that was the motivation, I wanted to make sure it succeeded. We wanted our kids to go and be safe and have a good experience in high school, which they did. But that's how everyone felt—we wanted to keep that school. We didn't want the race riots to be the reason that Poly met its demise. Everyone knew we had to keep the peace, we never once thought about moving, our roots were too strong here.*

The goal of the white parents was for Poly to be a safe place to send their kids, where they wouldn't be accidentally swept up in race-related violence. The goal of the black families, of course, was exactly the same.

The difference for the black community was that Barnes and Price and Butler weren't just thinking about their kids. They were aware that they needed to help prevent white flight as well.

"One of the first things we did was ask how can we retain as many white students as possible," said Barnes. "Across the country a lot of people didn't think about that. We all understood, though, that if you have white flight, pretty soon the school becomes segregated just by that action. The black community knew it was important that didn't happen—we didn't want our kids to be abandoned."

Having spent five years leading the PCIC as a voice for the black community to demand changes on campus, Barnes was also aware that having white voices leading the way would make the school district more amenable to changes.

"To make something like what we were doing work, you have to have somebody in the establishment, the majority, that's willing to solve it," he said.

> They had the power and they had the tradition—if you can find someone like that, it can work. And Nancy was that person. She wanted Poly to work, and she wanted it to work for everyone. Our rallying cry became to make sure Poly could become the best school that it could be. It was really a lofty goal, and it saved the school at the time.

The meetings were productive, creating the modern Poly and coming up with a number of programs that still make up pillars of the campus culture more than four decades later. But those solutions weren't inevitable conclusions: they were the result of tension and disagreements.

Angry parents would sometimes resort to standing on a table or yelling to make a point, and when the black members of the PCIC went to Bixby Knolls for a meeting, they sometimes did so warily. One husband of a black PCIC member stayed on the porch of the Latimers' house during a meeting with a gun under his coat in case anyone tried to rush the home. Latimer said she remembered when the PCIC had their first meetings at her house, she'd get calls afterward from concerned neighbors.

"We yelled, we cried, but we worked things out and got things settled," one anonymous black parent on the PCIC told the *Press-Telegram* in a story about the group.

The distance between parents in the PCIC occasionally spilled over into the public. In 1980, the *Press-Telegram* documented a disagreement between Latimer and Butler. Butler was a well-respected advocate not just for her work as a PCIC chair and leader but for heading Long Beach's recreation commission as well as being Poly's first black PTA president.

Amid growing frustration that the eighty-member PCIC was losing its effectiveness after more than a decade of existence, Latimer hosted a meeting of Bixby Knolls parents to discuss concerns in the neighborhood about Poly. Butler was upset that Latimer and the parents from the affluent neighborhood (all of whom were white, according to the *Press-Telegram* reporting) circumvented the PCIC.

"The situation finds two women who worked shoulder to shoulder to build the interracial committee now pitted against each other," said the *Press-Telegram* article.

Latimer said it wasn't intended as a separate, all-white meeting but rather a neighborhood meeting in a neighborhood that happened to be all white. Butler took her complaint to the NAACP, with Long Beach chapter president Frank Berry sending a letter of complaint to the school board.

Cohn agreed with Butler and said he was disappointed to learn that a side meeting had been called.

"The PCIC was the vehicle the board set up to handle problems like this. I think the NAACP's reaction was appropriate," Cohn told the *Press-Telegram*. "If you have strong feelings about black youngsters, you should be able to voice them openly. If it's violence they're worried about, well, there are people in the black community who are just as afraid of street crime as white parents."

Despite these kinds of differences, the PCIC was enormously successful in coming up with solutions and making recommendations to the board. They said they wanted an academic magnet on campus as a way of attracting and retaining white students. They wanted a program around Homecoming to help showcase the school's diversity as a strength, not a weakness. They wanted redevelopment of the neighborhood around the school, to help improve life off campus. And finally, they wanted a human relations camp that would take Poly students out of the city while they were still new to high school and teach them how to talk to one another and relate to one another, even if they came from different backgrounds.

Those programs all took hold and were enormously successful in the mid- to late 1970s, so that by the time Latimer and Butler's feud reached the newspaper, the campus was relatively quiet and content.

"The kids are great," said Latimer in the *Press-Telegram*. "They're doing fine. All the divisiveness is among the adults."

ISSUES ON CAMPUS REMAINED

While the PCIC was plugging away throughout the 1970s, tensions on campus eased. There were no more major eruptions of violence, no more big clashes between students. That didn't mean that issues didn't remain, however.

Poly's place in its community was still changing, and the neighborhood around the school was increasingly dangerous. Muir freshman football player Ricky Snowden was hit by a stray bullet while playing a game at Poly and died. Violent crime and theft around the school became commonplace, and many Poly students of the time have stories of being assaulted walking to or from school.

Students felt the weight of Snowden's death and lamented both his loss and the increasingly muddied reputation of their school. "Poly students were not responsible for the shooting," read that year's yearbook. "Outsiders caused and perpetuated a new reputation for Poly: the school where people get shot."

As the Vietnam War came to an end in 1975, Long Beach became home to a large influx of Vietnamese refugees as one of the top relocation options for the half-million refugees to come to America between 1975 and 2000. In the late 1970s and continuing for another two decades, there was a large immigration of Cambodian refugees fleeing the horrors of the Killing Fields.

With an additional increase in the number of Polynesian and Hispanic students, Poly's administration quickly went from trying to manage tensions between white and black students to managing a campus with students from all kinds of backgrounds, many of whom didn't speak English.

There was a growing number of ethnic classes offered by the school, including Black History, Minorities History, Asian Studies and Mexican Art and Culture. This diversity, of course, became one of Poly's hallmarks and greatest strengths, but it posed challenges in the 1970s that required action.

The Chicano Club on campus became a political force, protesting that the PCIC addressed concerns of white and black student, but not theirs. They wanted more Spanish-speaking staff, both among the ranks of teachers and administration.

According to a *Call-Enterprise* story from 1973, these protests made their way to the PCIC and the school board. "Barbara Garcia, a 17-year-old senior, told the board that the Chicano students are frustrated because they feel they have no one on campus to identify with or who understands their problems," said the article.

Rosemary Negron, a concerned parent who was a member of the PCIC, said that further conflict would be brewing if there weren't more bilingual classes and staff at Poly.

According to the article, "She said because their skin is brown, the Chicanos are treated as second-class citizens and 'the people of Long Beach are not going to take it anymore. This is not a threat, it's just a statement.'"

Negron also said that the PCIC "does not speak to the Spanish community at Poly."

Still, there was hope. The area around the school began redevelopment, as a few blocks of blight were cleared for a gated student parking lot up Atlantic Avenue, just south of Pacific Coast Highway. Plans were drawn up for the Poly Apartments, which were to provide secure and affordable housing adjacent to the school for inner-city families. The end of the Vietnam War broke the fever pitch of the nation's youth protests and also removed the looming threat of being drafted.

And while some may have been frustrated with the PCIC, the group's recommendations were crystalizing and beginning to go into effect, helping alleviate the problems of the 1960s and '70s and shaping the modern Poly.

PCIC'S CHANGES TAKE ROOT

The first major program recommended by the PCIC was what came to be known as Poly North, a human relations camp for first-year Poly students held over a weekend in the mountains. The first trip happened in 1975–76, led by Cohn.

"The challenge coming from some of us was, 'You're spending all this money on additional security at the school, what are you actually doing to make sure that youngsters get along?'" said Cohn. It was a question echoed by his friend Burcham. It was a fortunate coincidence that both men, future renowned education leaders, found themselves on the high school campus together early in their careers.

Both had initially gone to college with the goal of becoming clergymen, perhaps one reason they tended to take a holistic, human approach to mending Poly's rifts.

The PCIC went to the mountain retreat and designed a weekend curriculum, one still largely used at the Poly North trips that are still taken today with Poly sophomores. Once the program was in place, Cohn and the Poly sophomores went up for a weekend of discussion, human relations

POLY NORTH

Another long-running Poly tradition that emerged in the late 1970s was Poly North, a human relations camp in the mountains for the school's sophomore class. *Courtesy* Caerulea *archives*.

games and trust exercises. Fresh air and mountain scenery were intended to broaden the students' perspectives about the world.

"When the analysis came through on who participated in the riots, the kids who were the main participants were kids who felt alienated, not connected, that sort of thing," remembered Cohn. Because the school was tenth through twelfth grade at the time, the goal was to get a diverse group of sophomores up to the Poly North retreat to forge bonds that would help guide the school.

"From my point of view, it was a very successful experience in bringing kids together," said Cohn. "Everyone was on the same page about working actively to bring kids together."

Three years later, Mel Collins came from Hughes and replaced Cohn as the director of Poly North and as the head of the school's career center. Recent Poly alum Shawn Ashley was one of Collins's staff members at the camp in the late 1970s and early '80s, foreshadowing the duo's historically successful tenure at the school as co-principals two decades later.

The Poly North camp still runs today and has been directed for more than a decade by Rob Shock, a Poly alum who is also the boys' athletic director at the school.

PACE

One of the chief recommendations of the PCIC was a rigorous academic magnet program at Poly. Magnets had been tried before, including the School of Educational Alternatives, an eighty-student pilot program at Poly that never caught on, largely due to its lack of structure and a curriculum that wasn't challenging enough.

The solution was the Program of Additional Curricular Experiences—a new college prep program that could admit students from all over the city, not just from the Poly area.

"When I look at PACE, I am amazed," said Cohn in a recent interview. "Most urban school districts, if you told families we are going to locate the top academic program in the heart of the inner-city, and if you want that for your child, this is where they're going to go, they'd laugh at you and say, 'Where do I sign the petition to recall the school board?'"

The program was the brainchild and in some ways the baby of Dr. Nancy Gray, a comparative literature teacher at Poly at the time. Gray was on the PCIC, and after one meeting in Poly's faculty lounge behind the cafeteria, Principal Jack DuBois pulled her aside.

"We need a magnet program," he said. "We want you to figure out what to do and do it. Do you have any ideas?"

Gray said she was wary at first, having been in the district long enough to know she needed support behind a big project like that. She had philosophical backing but would end up needing to do most of the grunt work herself.

Nancy Gray, the founder and director of PACE, Poly's award-winning academic magnet. *Courtesy* Caerulea *archives.*

"I started researching everywhere I could find," she said. "Hunter College High School in New York was a loose model—they could arrange around science and math, or liberal arts or visual arts. I thought that would work if I could staff it."

Gray created a modified block schedule for PACE that would allow the kids to take extra classes. Then she had to do the hard part: sell something completely new to parents, many of whom had never even considered sending their kids to Poly. "How were we going to sell the parents? A lot of the East Long Beach kids wanted to go to Poly, but their parents were worried they'd be murdered before lunch. So I thought, 'What do I give these parents?' The answer was AP classes—a way to save money on their kids' college education."

Advanced Placement classes were a way for students to earn college credit while they were still in high school. They're quite common now and offered at most high schools, but that wasn't yet the case in the mid-'70s. PACE offered AP classes by the bucketload, and it was common then (and now) for students to graduate from high school with as much as a full year of college credit already accumulated.

Gray went out recruiting at all fourteen Long Beach junior high schools, many of which were openly hostile to her cause, scheduling her talks during classes or lunchtime assemblies when students were less likely to come listen to her.

"At one school the principal sat down and played jazz while I was giving my presentation, at another I arrived at a school and the lights were down on the stage with electricians hammering on it during the assembly," she said.

Gray's charge from the PCIC and the school was clear: make the magnet as attractive as possible, especially to white parents. She said she was given numbers showing that the year before PACE started, the incoming class of new students had only nineteen white female students among their ranks.

"That's why the emphasis from the beginning was to really get out hard and recruit all those schools in East Long Beach," said Gray.

PACE has since grown into a nationally recognized powerhouse and a model for inner-city college prep programs, making it hard to believe how difficult it was for Gray to get the program off the ground. The response to her message was strong, as a crush of parents tried to sign their kids up. Meanwhile, Gray had to spend the 1975–76 school year running the PACE program as its founder and counselor while also teaching classes in comparative literature, AP European history, French and Spanish. When she went on recruiting trips that took her out of the classroom, she stayed up late the night before recording her lectures onto a tape recorder for the substitute teacher to play in class the next day.

After a year of teaching six classes, Principal Ed Eveland finally started building a support staff around Gray. Meanwhile, the program got stronger each year.

"After a few years we started getting applications from the children of the teachers in the East Long Beach schools who'd fought tooth and nail to get rid of us," Gray said with a laugh. Soon, Ivy League schools along with Stanford and Occidental began regularly stopping by to talk to Gray.

PACE was such a success that Greta McGree would soon launch CIC as another on-campus magnet. The two programs quickly provided the attraction that the PCIC had hoped for, pulling the best students from all over the city. The academic magnets were not only the right idea—they were run by the right people. (For more on the history of the academic magnets and their impact on the school, see chapter 19.)

INTERNATIONAL AMBASSADORS

If there was one turning point in the history of Long Beach Poly, one moment when it was clear the school was going to overcome the strife of the late 1960s and early '70s, it might have been the Homecoming week of the 1976 football season.

The theme of the celebration was "Spirit Comes in All Colors," a message specifically intended to celebrate Poly's diversity. In the buildup to the Homecoming game, there were different cultural dance presentations on the rally stage at lunchtime. Then, at the game that Friday night, the school introduced its newest tradition.

It had been five years since Poly did away with Homecoming queens and kings; this was the year they unveiled its replacement.

"In lieu of a Homecoming queen and court, our first International Ambassadors made their debut this year," reads that year's *Caerulea*. "Chosen to represent their ethnic groups, the six seniors officiated at such functions as Homecoming and the Intercultural Fair. Hopefully this will continue as a tradition befitting a truly diverse school."

Indeed it has. In the earliest years of the International Ambassadors, the group was made up of race-specific honorees. There were male and female representatives for the white student body, the black student body, the Hispanic students and the Asian students.

Over the years, the method of choosing International Ambassadors has changed. There are now time-intensive service projects and high academic components to the honor. What hasn't changed is Poly's dedication to trying something new and staking a claim to what the school was supposed to be about. Instead of a simple popularity contest, the school has for more than forty years chosen to hold up examples of its diversity, as well as its character.

"I CARE ABOUT POLY"

The PCIC's recommendations, outlined in the previous sections, provided tangible, significant structural changes to the school and how it would be operated, both by the administration and by student leaders.

That wasn't the only thing responsible for leading Poly out of the wilderness—the leadership of its principals was enormously significant as well. In addition to those mentioned above, Ed Eveland and Bob Ellis were important figures in the school's history in the 1970s and early 1980s.

Eveland took the job in '76 as many of the aforementioned changes were being made and took it upon himself to help smooth the transition between Poly's past and its future. He quoted biblical scripture in his welcome message that fall.

"The 84th Psalm speaks of a desert generation that passed through the Valley of Weeping. The prophet challenged the Pilgrims to make it a place of Springs, changing the assaults of fate into achievement. It offers inspiration to every generation that lives through a period of difficulty and challenge," he wrote.

Buttons reading "I Care About Poly" and "I Am Somebody At Poly" were printed and handed out to students. Homecoming themes and Intercultural Fairs continued to emphasize that students should be proud of their school's diversity, not fearful of it. "Poly Faces From Many Places" was one; "The Poly Experience" was another.

The students responded. Things got better.

Not only was there a distinct lack of on-campus violence, but morale was high as well. The yearbooks were once again filled with starry-eyed missives penned by romantic soon-to-be-graduates.

"The unity that we feel stems from sharing a common experience—the Poly experience," read one such *Caerulea* introduction.

> *It is easy to find our differences, the most apparent being our individual ethnic descent. But we look for our similarities.... [I]t has been stated that the main purpose of high school is to prepare one for life. What better preparation could there possibly be for the mainstream of life than intercultural interaction? So although we are many, we are one. All of our colors blend together to form just two: green and gold.*

Dance instructor Mary Ellen Over supervised a diverse group that performed frequently around campus. In the spring of 1977, the campus hosted its first Community Picnic, welcoming church groups and neighbors for a cookout in the quad that included barbecued ribs, teriyaki chicken, lumpia and chili dogs.

The passage of Title IX in 1972 slowly made for big changes, as well. When the CIF and the Moore League added girls' sports in full in the mid-1970s, it created a whole new world for Poly to dominate athletically. Female students were also allowed into the JROTC for the first time, and suddenly on the sidelines of big sporting events, the school mascot Jonathan Jackrabbit was joined by Jacqueline Jackrabbit.

THE CHAMPIONSHIP SPIRIT

Throughout the school's history, the general well-being and spirit of Poly's campus have always been tied to its sports programs. It's hard to say which is the chicken or the egg, but it's true that the fall after the 1972 riots was the only winless season in Poly football history. It's also true that as the campus was beginning to get its groove back in the late 1970s, the golden hardware began to flow again.

There was the CIF football championship in 1980, the school's first since the late 1950s. Then in 1984, coach Ron Palmer guided the school's basketball team to a CIF, state and national championship. Another football championship came in 1985.

These weren't the only honors flooding Poly's way. The PACE program, now joined by the CIC magnet, was turning out National Merit Scholars, and by the early 1980s Poly was offering more Advanced Placement classes than any high school west of the Mississippi.

The PCIC continued to meet on a monthly basis in the faculty lounge, but it was becoming less and less necessary. The programs it had recommended flourished and became the new representatives for the school: the International Ambassadors were interviewed on regional radio and television stations and featured in newspapers as role models for how to help a school recover from racial strife.

A ROSE THROUGH CONCRETE

On New Year's Eve, the day before 1975 passed into 1976, Eveland was in his office. Change was underway at Poly, and he was confident that it would take hold and that the school would come out of the dark tunnel and back into the light.

That day, he wrote a memo to W. Odie Wright, a Poly alum who was also the LBUSD superintendent at the time. The interdepartmental memorandum was a simple enough request: he wanted 150 rose plants to put into the planters in Poly's quad.

He had the idea that the roses would be tended to by the students of Marc Fortain, Poly's science department head. He also had the idea that the garden would signify that Poly was different from other schools who'd been torn apart, with half of their population fleeing in fear of the other half.

"The roses—especially during the eight or nine months of blooming—would make the campus a real show piece," wrote Eveland.

Not many inner-city high schools can boast a well-tended rose garden in their quad. Not many schools have ever endured what Poly did and come out stronger, either.

8

YEARS OF GROWTH, CENTENNIAL, 1986–1995

I n the latter half of the 1980s, the sailing was pretty smooth for Poly, certainly compared to the turbulence of the late 1960s and 1970s. The school had reestablished itself as a statewide sports powerhouse and had become a national academic force as well thanks to PACE and CIC.

In the late 1980s and early '90s, the campus became truly integrated, as PACE and CIC students came to Poly full time. For several years, the magnet students had the option of attending Poly for half the day before returning to their home schools to take the remainder of their classes and participate in sports and elective activities.

The effect of bringing those students on campus full time was profound. Brett Alexander got to see both sides of the change, as a student and a teacher. The son of Bill Alexander, a longtime Poly teacher and activities director, Brett graduated in '85, started teaching at Poly in '93 and has been the *Caerulea* advisor since 2003.

"I'm fortunate enough to say I was here when PACE and CIC students stopped leaving Poly, and our music programs, our drama programs, our sports programs all grew," he said. "There was one drama class, now there's five. There were a few music classes, now there are a dozen."

The city's love for the school and its traditions had never gone away, and now that the campus was stable with excellent athletic, academic and music programs in place to draw from all over town, a stream of talented students in every discipline began to flood Poly.

Consider that from 1986 to 1990, the school's student body included rappers Snoop Dogg and Nate Dogg, banda and ranchera legend Jenni Rivera, Sublime frontman Bradley Nowell and rock/jazz keyboardist Ikey Owens (who became a GRAMMY winner after playing with the Mars Volta and Jack White). Within a decade of their graduations from high school, that diverse group of black, Hispanic and white musicians would dominate the airwaves. As Snoop Dogg has often pointed out, what made Poly a unique breeding ground for talent was its diversity, along with the fact that those musicians were listening to and influenced by the variety of cultural music around them.

The world loved what it heard—those musicians alone would go on to sell more than seventy-one million albums.

Actresses Cameron Diaz and Tiffani-Amber Thiessen were students at this time as well, and Diaz, who was a cheerleader her freshman year, said the experience of the school was unique to anything she's seen since. "To me, it speaks to the diversity of Long Beach, the location of Poly is the epicenter, where all these different cultures intersect," she said.

Andy Osman and Chris Stevens were establishing the school's award-winning music program, which they'd go on to guide for more than three decades. At the same time, athletes like Willie McGinest were taking advantage of everything the school had to offer. A football star who went

Willie McGinest is arguably the finest football player to ever come out of Poly, with multiple Super Bowl rings and Pro Bowl honors. *Courtesy* Caerulea *archives.*

on to be a top-five draft pick and a three-time Super Bowl champion, McGinest was also in Poly's CIC magnet, where he was a 4.0 student.

"I'd always been a good student, and I'd always known that Poly was the mecca for sports," said McGinest. "That meant so much to me to have a place that offered the best of the best in both."

All of this success meant that the PCIC's purpose changed—its mission had been largely fulfilled. Rather than trying to come up with innovative new ways to meet crises, the group served as a sounding board to hear student complaints and a fundraising arm, as the PCIC and PTA raised money for a new rally stage in 1986. Yearbook photos of the PCIC show that a formal group that regularly had seventy-five to one hundred people at its meetings had dwindled to a group of just ten by the late 1980s.

The big names at Poly didn't just happen to be there, either. They were actively participating in Poly's specialized programs. Athletes like McGinest were in magnet programs, musicians like Owens and Rivera were playing music in Poly's bands and even Snoop Dogg was testing his lyrical skills while attending Poly North.

Rob Shock is Poly's longtime athletic director and director of Poly North, and the 1987 Poly grad was already volunteering at the camp by the time Snoop attended as a sophomore. "At that time nobody knew those guys would be who they are obviously," he said. "Snoop got in trouble at camp—the kids all do skits and he rapped during his, and I believe he said some words he wasn't supposed to say."

"AS CROWDED AS DISNEYLAND"

In 1990, the Long Beach Unified School District moved ninth grade from the junior high schools to the high schools, making Poly a four-year campus. The result was an additional 900 students at Poly, bringing enrollment up to 3,600 and drawing comparisons to Disneyland in a *High Life* editorial. Over the next five years, demand around Long Beach for students to attend Poly continued to swell, and the school would reach an enrollment of more than 4,000 by its centennial celebration in 1995.

Wayne Piercy, who was principal from 1985 to 1991, was, like his predecessor, a Poly alum. When he retired following the 1991 school year, the district broke with recent tradition and did not look to its own ranks to select whoever the most qualified Poly alum happened to be. Instead, Poly area superintendent Carl Cohn—who would become LBUSD superintendent the next year—decided to lead a national search.

"I decided not to do the typical Long Beach thing, I decided I'm going to get the best available person in the country and have them come to Poly," said Cohn. He ended up hiring HJ Green from Tulsa, Oklahoma, a white principal who had helped integrate Booker T. Washington High School in Tulsa.

"Nobody but me had seen him, so when they heard his name was HJ Green, everybody thought he was black," said Cohn. "HJ is as white as Will Rogers. Everybody was already pissed off that I went outside of Long Beach, so when he finally shows up it kind of compounded. 'He went out

Above: The end-of-day flag retreat in front of the school in 1924. *Courtesy* Caerulea *archives.*

Right: An early photo of the Poly JROTC color guard, one of the first of its kind in California. *Courtesy* Caerulea *archives.*

Shot from inside a classroom after the 1933 earthquake. The roof is collapsed, but the light fixture is still attached. *From Poly historical archives.*

The front of the old Poly campus, with the famous dome collapsed after the 1933 earthquake. *From Poly historical archives.*

An overhead look at the total devastation from the 1933 earthquake at Poly. Every school in Long Beach was destroyed. *From Poly historical archives.*

After the earthquake destroyed the school, classes met daily on the campus's Burcham Field until tents could be put up. *From Poly historical archives.*

Left: Flag raising in front of the "new" (and current) campus in 1936. The familiar copper "Enter to Learn, Go Forth to Serve" sign has already been installed. *Courtesy* Caerulea *archives*.

Below: Overlooking the quad in 1937 as the Poly campus was being rebuilt. The building depicted is the administration building still used today. In the background are oil derricks on Signal Hill. *Courtesy* Caerulea *archives*.

A display case in the current administration building depicting historic Poly items from before the earthquake including bricks and other rubble from the destroyed buildings. *Photo by Stephen Carr.*

"Speed Is the Greatest Factor In Modern Life" reads this historic Catalina tile mosaic, built as part of the WPA program in 1935. *Photo by Stephen Carr.*

Above: *Industrial Activities in Long Beach*, another historic mural built as part of the WPA program. Jean Swiggett and Ivan Bartlett painted this scene of Long Beach's bustling waterfront in 1938–39. It is currently preserved in a sealed stairwell in the 400 building and can only be seen through glass. *Photo by Stephen Carr.*

Left: Poly's flagpole at the center of the quad, present day. The columns are excavated remains of the original campus's columns, destroyed in the earthquake. *Photo by Stephen Carr.*

Supreme Service; a plaque dedicated to the Poly alums who died at war. It's hanging in the lobby of Poly's library. *Photo by Stephen Carr.*

Perhaps Poly's most accomplished alum, Billie Jean King, pictured here with student body president Bill J. Penn, returned home to be honored by Poly in 1969. *Courtesy* Caerulea *archives.*

Top: Gene Washington, a football star and a leader on campus in the 1960s. Washington poses with the gavel after being voted student body president in 1965. *Courtesy* Caerulea *archives.*

Left: Carl Cohn: an important figure in Poly's history, first as a counselor in the 1970s and later as the Long Beach Unified School District's superintendent. Pictured here in 1975. *Courtesy* Caerulea *archives.*

Poly Community Interracial Committee

A meeting of the Poly Community Interracial Committee in 1973; the PCIC recommended strategies that saved the school and birthed the modern Poly. *Courtesy* Caerulea *archives.*

Poly's 1976 CIF championship basketball team, coached by the legendary Ron Palmer. Baseball Hall of Famer Tony Gwynn is holding the ball; standouts Mike Wiley, Johnny Nash and James Hughes are in the back. *Courtesy* Caerulea *archives.*

Right: John Atkinson skies for a dunk in 1981. Atkinson has since been an assistant coach on dozens of CIF championship Poly basketball and track teams. *Courtesy* Caerulea *archives.*

Below: Samoan dancers draw a crowd at the Poly Intercultural Fair in 1979. *Courtesy* Caerulea *archives.*

A display of an old Jonathan Jackrabbit mascot with Poly's trophies and the 1919 championship football banner in the school's Hall of Fame. *Courtesy* Caerulea *archives.*

Right: The famous shot of actress Cameron Diaz when she was a cheerleader at Poly in 1988. *Courtesy* Caerulea *archives.*

Below: One of Poly's most well-known alums, Snoop Dogg, has often returned to the school to give back. He also occasionally uses it as a backdrop, as in this album cover art for *Ego Trippin'*, taken on Jackrabbit Lane. *Author's collection.*

The first half of Poly's centennial mural, featuring the original Poly campus building and several prominent teachers and administrators from the early days. *Photo by Stephen Carr.*

The second half of Poly's centennial mural, featuring three-time Long Beach mayor Beverly O'Neill, Tony Gwynn and other prominent Poly alums. *Photo by Stephen Carr.*

"Home of the Jackrabbits": the exterior of Poly's gymnasium. *Photo by Stephen Carr.*

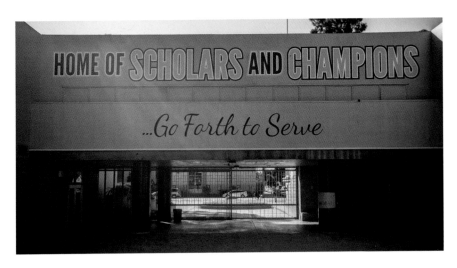

As students leave out of the front of the school, they get a look at two of Poly's famous mottos. *Photo by Stephen Carr.*

Above: The mural in Poly's library emphasizes the school's commitment to diversity, a major part of Poly's history. *Photo by Stephen Carr.*

Right: Legendary track and football coach Don Norford embraces future Olympian Bryshon Nellum after a world championship run at the Penn Relays in 2007. *Photo by Kirby Lee.*

Poly has produced more than sixty NFL alums, the most of any high school in America. Some of their jerseys hang alongside other trophies in a display case in the administration building. *Photo by Stephen Carr.*

Left: Ariana Washington made California and Poly history with six individual state championships as a sprinter before going on to NCAA titles at Oregon and then the Olympics. Here, she throws up two "Jackrabbits" as she crosses the finish line after her final high school race in 2014. *Photo by Kirby Lee.*

Right: David Burcham in 1919. Burcham is a Poly legend and was the school's principal from 1907 until 1941, the longest tenure of anyone in school history. *Courtesy* Caerulea *archives.*

and got somebody from another place and he's a white guy! What is wrong with Carl Cohn?'"

Green would become one of the school's most popular principals among both students and other administrators, with a southern charm that won over just about everybody.

"A month or so after he started everybody is patting me on the back going, 'Carl, that was a brilliant selection,'" said Cohn with a laugh.

GREEN'S NEW DEAL

Under Green, the school's special programs continued to flourish. PACE produced a then-record eight National Merit Scholars in 1991. Green noticed that PACE and CIC students had more pride in their academic standing than other students, so he oversaw the creation of "small learning communities" like PAC-RIM and Beach, making sure that all students felt like they were a part of a special curriculum.

The innovative educator said there were a lot of similarities between the school he ran in Oklahoma and Poly, but a lot of differences, too.

"The size of the school was pretty shocking. I had been a principal of a school of 2,400 and we thought that was a giant school," said Green. "You come to Poly and it's 4,000 students and that was a surprise. Another thing was the diversity. In Oklahoma we were primarily a biracial school, black and white. At Poly there were and still are basically six distinct ethnic groups there."

Poly's large Southeast Asian population makes it unique. As the Killing Fields genocide raged in Cambodia and refugees fled to other nearby countries, Long Beach's First Friends Church was one of the first to reach out. Cambodian refugees who'd fled to Thailand found a welcome home in Long Beach through the First Friends connection, and thousands arrived quickly. The church has long since been giving two sets of sermons, one in English and one in Khmer.

"The first wave wasn't necessarily coming here," said Vincent Puth, a Cambodian Poly alum who is now the school's activities director. "But then everyone's brother or grandma was in Long Beach. Everyone had to come here, we were starting a new community."

There was already a heavy gang presence in the neighborhood, and a booming Cambodia Town full of refugees stepped into that fray, with Cambodian and Vietnamese gangs popping up as a way for the city's new residents to protect themselves.

As the influence of street gangs in Long Beach increased throughout the 1980s and '90s, Poly became a sanctuary from the violence that often lay just outside the school's gates. While the 1970s had seen students afraid to come to school, the 1990s saw students fearful to leave it.

"One thing about Poly for decades is if it's 7:00 a.m. to 5:00 p.m., it's safe here," said Puth. "Everyone says that, people of any race. You have a Poly sweater on, you're walking down MLK and you make that left turn, you're safe. That hit home for a lot of people—the school is a sanctuary."

Gang strife between Asian and Hispanic gangs was particularly fierce, which left students who weren't involved in gangs exposed, with the very real possibility of being confronted or challenged because of their race if they were in the wrong neighborhood.

"The Cambodian refugee population was a mixture of students from very different educational backgrounds," said Green. "A number of students who had very minimal or no education, but by the same token a number of students whose parents were high-level professionals in Cambodia. Some of our top PACE students were refugees from Cambodia."

On campus, Green's staff was committed to quieting any issues between Pacific Islander, Asian, black and Hispanic gangs.

"The students, even the ones involved in gangs, were supportive of that," said Green. "They didn't want things to get crazy on campus either. Many of the Cambodian students would stay on campus for hours after school. They didn't want to leave because they knew if there was any danger to them it was out in the neighborhood. They'd stay in the quad after school—I think all of us felt that Poly was a safe haven."

While the neighborhood around Poly became known nationally as a major hotbed of gang activity, activity that was chronicled by Snoop Dogg and Nate Dogg and other rappers, the campus remained a neutral zone, often because of explicit truces and agreements.

"Many times I've seen a student who's involved go up to someone and stop something from happening," said Keith Anderson, a longtime assistant coach at the school. "They'll say, 'Not here, take that off campus.' There's an understanding that the neighborhood stays in the neighborhood, and the school is a safe place."

Green said that he was impressed with the job that the school had done in overcoming its past struggles.

"The thing that was very unique about Poly was the pride that people had in the school," said Green. "There was a pride and a determination to hold it together. That made the difference. When I was there, what I noticed is that students were going out of their way to try to integrate the other groups."

Green said that the pride in the school was obvious to him when he came out to interview and first saw the rose garden in the quad.

"That to me was kind of symbolic of the pride that people who worked there and went to school there had," he said. "That you could have that kind of a rose garden right in the middle of an inner-city school."

RODNEY KING RIOTS AND ACE OF SPADES KILLING

While Poly had responded to the Southern California–wide racial strife of the early 1970s in a way that was constructive and ameliorative, the same was not true of the rest of the region. For anyone who'd been living under a rock and didn't already know that, it became painfully clear after a "not guilty" verdict was returned at the conclusion of the Rodney King trial, in which four police officers were acquitted of assault and excessive force despite video evidence of them brutally beating King.

On April 29, 1992, after the verdict was announced, riots flared up around Southern California for six days. Over $1 billion of property damage was done, with sixty-three people killed in the riots and more than two thousand injured. There were more than twelve thousand arrests. The riots were immortalized in a song by Sublime, titled "April 29, 1992," written by Poly alum Bradley Nowell.

Some of this violence spread to other campuses in Long Beach. The *LA Times* reported that two hundred students at Wilson were involved in a "racially motivated brawl." At Poly, things were calm, but just off campus it looked like a war zone. Businesses near the campus burned down or were looted, and Long Beach officials decided to close schools until things calmed down.

On Friday evening at Pacific Coast Highway and Lemon, just a few blocks east of Poly, a man was dragged off his motorcycle and fatally shot in the head. The city implemented an emergency curfew as more than one hundred National Guard troops and an additional two hundred marines arrived to help more than three hundred police officers try to restore order. In all, more than five hundred were arrested in Long Beach, with more than three hundred fires having been set.

At Poly, administrators shook their head at the devastation off campus but also thanked their lucky stars that the campus was spared.

JACKRABBIT SPOTLIGHT: CRYSTAL IRVING

A trailblazer from a family of trailblazers, Crystal Irving was a runner at Poly who graduated in 1988 and went on to star at Long Beach City College and UNLV before a pro career on the track. Irving's father was the first black owner of a gas station in Long Beach, and her mother and grandmother owned a senior home.

"We've defeated the odds where we haven't always had the best education, but we work hard," said Irving. "A lot of kids don't have that backing, and I know it, so I valued any help I got and I try to help out however I can."

Irving has been a huge help. She arrived at Poly as a coach in 1997 and has been at Poly for more than two decades since. She was the school's first female athletic director, overseeing the girls' sports program. She also became the school's first female track and field head coach after Don Norford's retirement in 2014, having served as his top assistant for fifteen years. She became the first woman at Poly to be the head coach on a state championship team a few years after taking over the track program and is also believed to be the only woman to be a head coach of a boys' team at Poly, as the head coach of both the boys' and girls' program.

"It's important that the kids that go to Poly see someone that's successful, that comes from the same place," said Irving. "I grew up down the street, off MLK."

Irving ran for Norford and coached under him and has continued the Poly tradition of having a staff made up of long-tenured alums and volunteers. Her dedication to Poly is so great that she turned down the head coaching position at UNLV to remain as a coach and athletic director with the Jackrabbits.

Earlier that year, the Ace of Spades murder case made headlines across California, as three Poly students were charged in the murder of another. The students charged had been running a small gang out of the school's JROTC program, committing vandalism and stealing from cars off-campus. The murdered student was a member of the group, named the Ace of Spades, and reportedly cooperated with police in an investigation into their activities, prompting one of the leaders of the gang to set up an execution-style killing in which he was beaten, stabbed, choked with barbed wire and then thrown over a cliff in San Pedro.

The murder of a student and subsequent arrests of another three students for his killing shocked what had become a relatively quiet campus.

CENTENNIAL CELEBRATION

As Poly marched toward its centennial anniversary, things were looking rosy under Green's guidance. In order to accommodate the larger number of students, the school decided to beef up its administration. Maggie Webster and Karen Hilburn joined Green as co-principals in 1993, and the school has had at least two principals ever since.

Webster and Hilburn were the first women to serve as principals at the school, and Webster was the first African American principal as well—in the more than two decades since, the school has always had a black co-principal.

The new faces in the principals' office weren't the only new look on campus, as the three-story $5 million science building opened in 1993 as well. The nation had begun to take notice of Poly's innovative ideas, a trend that would really pick up in the latter half of the 1990s. Kerrill Kephart and Huong Tran Nguyen were both honored by Disney with the National Teacher of the Year award, bringing an even brighter spotlight to Poly.

The centennial celebration in the fall of 1995 was a spectacular affair. A skywriter made a "100" cloud overhead, and the school's centennial mural was unveiled, after having been painted by students over the better part of the previous school year. The mural depicted the 100-year history of the school with scenes from Poly's past—the mural changes from black and white to color and includes several famous Poly alums.

A time capsule that had been buried more than a half-century prior in the quad was dug up—it was filled with old newspapers, rubble from the earthquake and other artifacts.

Poly alum Beverly O'Neill was Long Beach's mayor at that time and gave a speech at the event, and she presented a congratulatory letter from President Bill Clinton.

"Poly gave me a lot of strength," said O'Neill in a recent interview with the authors. "Poly seems like the one place in the city that didn't need help building pride. Our challenges strengthened us."

Huong Nguyen and Kerrill Kephart were both named Disney National Teachers of the Year during the 1990s. *Courtesy* Caerulea *archives.*

The centennial celebration was met with a special section in the *Press-Telegram* celebrating Poly's history, and all agreed that the event—organized by Poly alum, teacher, historian and coach Sam Dimas—was a big success. It capped off with the renaming of Seventeenth Street as Jackrabbit Lane.

With a proud history and national recognition, Poly was ready to enter the new century and take its place among America's most famous and well-respected public schools.

9

POLY THE POWERHOUSE, 1996–PRESENT

I n the fall of 1997, as the new school year started, the superintendent of the Long Beach Unified School District was Carl Cohn. Poly's principals, paired for the first time, were Shawn Ashley and Mel Collins.

All three had been at Poly during the unrest of 1972—Cohn and Collins as young, energetic employees and Ashley as a senior student. The three of them now presided over a campus that had come out into the sunshine, with more than 4,500 students enrolled and hundreds more who would have come if there'd been room.

Ashley was hired in the fall of '96 and was co-principal with Maggie Webster for a year before Collins joined him. Ashley would go on to serve as Poly principal for fifteen years, a tenure exceeded only by the legendary David Burcham. Ashley was beloved by Poly's teachers and administrators for his hands-on approach and frequent encouraging notes. He was well liked by students in part because every year he made it a point to memorize the names and faces of every Poly student so he could greet them all in person.

Ironically, although he came to be synonymous with his alma mater, Ashley didn't want the job when Cohn offered it to him. He was serving as the principal at Washington Middle School a few blocks west of Poly, and that was where he said he wanted to stay.

"I didn't want to go," Ashley said.

To me, it was like trying to change the direction of a runaway train. Carl asked me a second time, and I figured I'd better not say no again. It didn't

Shawn Ashley (*left*) and Mel Collins, the powerhouse duo who helped lift Poly to a position of national prominence in the late 1990s. *Courtesy* Caerulea *archives.*

take much time for me to get on campus and realize that high school kids were just bigger kids. And I was smart enough to not want to make a bunch of changes at Poly just because I thought it was a good idea.

For a decade and a half, Ashley was a constant fixture at every Poly home sporting event, every concert, every dance event. He not only learned everyone's name but also dove into the daily life of the campus.

"That was the other thing that stopped me from wanting to go to Poly at first. I knew how many nights I'd be out and away from my family," he said. "But I also thought that if I was going to do this job right, to the level I wanted to do it, that's kind of the price you pay."

Ashley was right to not work too hard on changing the course of the school. By the mid-1990s, Poly's dominance had been established. What he focused on was putting the right people in the right places and giving them the resources they needed to be successful. For example, he approached boys' volleyball coach Carl Buggs about becoming the girls' basketball coach, something Buggs was initially hesitant about. After Ashley talked him into it, Buggs went on to win six state championships (and counting), a California record for the state's highest division.

Ashley's biggest focus was in settling down the flare-ups in violence between Cambodian and Hispanic gangs. The conflict was severe enough that the *New York Times* sent war correspondent Seth Mydans to cover it. Long Beach Police estimated that there were sixty drive-by shootings in the Poly neighborhood in the span of a year and a half, and Mydans quoted Song Kamsath, director of the Boys and Girls Club of Long Beach, as saying, "It's just like in a war zone. Everybody is scared."

The police estimates of the time were that there were 8,800 gang members in Long Beach, 4,000 of whom were Hispanic, with about 800 Cambodians involved. That number inverted at Poly, where there was a much larger Southeast Asian influence at the time; the ongoing conflict occasionally bled over onto Poly's campus and led Ashley to make a bargain.

"Some of the Asian gangs had made a real effort to get rid of Latino kids—if a Latino kid checked into school, by noon he would've been in a fight with an Asian kid," said Ashley. "I knew where the kids hung out and I'd go over and talk to the group. I had a new policy that if there was a fight between a Latino student and an Asian student, the Asian student was gone. And for the most part that quieted things down quickly."

It helped matters that when Ashley and Collins were running Poly together, Cohn was in the superintendent's office. Cohn had spent time working with the LBUSD's anti-gang task force and knew the lay of the land, as well as some of the specific challenges of the Poly area. He also believed in the power of Poly's story and what the school had overcome and was determined to make sure the school had whatever resources it needed to remain nationally relevant. Cohn asserted,

> *Poly and the Long Beach schools are responsible for the changing view of Long Beach from when Seth Mydans was reporting on this gritty port city to this dramatic turnaround that, in my judgment, endures to today....On the urban landscape, this is one of a kind, where the school system was vitally involved in the overall turnaround of the community.*

ATHLETIC, ACADEMIC, MUSICAL DOMINANCE

One of the biggest challenges facing the school was that it simply wasn't big enough. The enrollment reached nearly five thousand students in the early 2000s but was well over four thousand throughout the '90s and 2000s. That was one of the reasons for the opening of PAAL, a smaller, satellite campus offshoot of Poly. (See chapter 17 for more on PAAL.)

JACKRABBIT SPOTLIGHT: VINCENT PUTH

Few Poly alums represent the joyful diversity of the era better than Vincent Puth, the 2000 ASB president and a young leader in Long Beach's Cambodian community. Puth, a CIC alum who went from Poly to UC Berkeley for college, has since returned to Poly as a teacher, a co-director at Poly North and now as the school's activities director.

Puth's family owned Cambodia Town institution Mary's Video at Walnut and Anaheim, and he grew up rewinding cassette tapes in the store while attending elementary school. His parents fled the violence of the Khmer Rouge in Cambodia, escaping to Thailand before eventually coming to America. Long Beach is home to the largest Cambodian population anywhere in the world outside of Cambodia, and Puth said the community faced a number of challenges in Long Beach.

"Especially in my generation there was a big transition," he said.

Some of those challenges, like trying to establish an economic center, are common to first- and second-generation immigrants. Others, like dealing with gang violence and the PTSD associated with fleeing a genocide, were specific to the time and place.

"When I was growing up there were a lot of fights with Latino gangs or black gangs, " said Puth. "I grew up on Gundry and Peterson, and if you made a left and went a block, there were Longos [a Hispanic gang] who would jump you. If you make a right toward Poly, there's Rollin 20s [a black gang] and they'd just say what's up."

As a peace developed between Cambodian/Filipino gangs and the Rollin 20s and Insane Crips, that became another force driving the Cambodian community toward Poly.

"They weren't jumping us, so since the influence at Poly was more of the black gangs in the '80s and '90s, that was another reason we saw Poly as a home campus," said Puth. "Now the racial aspect of violence has been mostly taken away, but our community still sees Poly as the safe place because it's our home school, it's right on the north edge of Cambodia Town, and you can walk there."

Puth was one of those students who walked to school, and he's made his impact. Students went crazy when he was elected ASB president and c-walked on stage. Since graduating from Poly and Berkeley, he's become a leader in the Poly community.

"For me what made this school unique and connected was the teachers here really know who their students are, my teachers always made a point to include our culture in the classroom and make us feel validated," he said. "Some people had Cambodian art on the wall, the teachers would come buy Cambodian food at the Intercultural Fair. It's the best of the best."

Puth said that the school has kept its commitment to his community going with hires like himself, staffer/volleyball coach Vuthy Cheav and athletic director Rob Shock, who is half Filipino. He added,

A lot of Southeast Asian cultures, seeking assistance isn't done, you just truck along, keep it going. And a lot of these parents will shut down when they're talking to certain people. But they're more comfortable opening up to me or Rob. There wasn't any ego from the administration about that, they just wanted to make sure their families were taken care of.

Rooms that had been built as storage facilities ended up hosting small classes, and bungalows went up between the football and baseball fields. The *Caerulea* expanded to more than four hundred pages. The quad was so filled at lunch that no Poly alum of that era has ever struggled to maneuver through a crowd since.

The demand made sense—Poly was the place to be in Long Beach. The school was having its most successful sports decade ever, winning thirty CIF championships and eight state championships in a ten-year period from 1996 to 2005. The school renamed its baseball field after the Gwynn family, and the football team was on TV frequently, playing in three consecutive CIF championships against big-moneyed private school Mater Dei.

In 2001, the Poly football program had a moment. The team was ranked No. 1 in the nation and appeared on the cover of the *LA Times*, and it is still the only high school team in history with five first-team *Parade* All-Americans. The Jackrabbits faced De La Salle in the first-ever meeting

As part of a record-setting stretch of five consecutive CIF championship appearances, Poly's football team was honored on ABC's Monday Night Football. *Courtesy* Caerulea *archives.*

of the top two high school teams in the nation, which was also the first nationally televised high school football game; a meeting so momentous it drew eighteen thousand fans to Veterans Memorial Stadium in Long Beach. The game was immortalized in a book by alum Don Wallace.

The Jackrabbits were coached by a Poly product, Raul Lara, and featured several future NFL talents, including Marcedes Lewis, Winston Justice, Manuel Wright and Darnell Bing. The team was a perfect representation of the school, an underdog turned powerhouse, with a Hispanic head coach and a racially diverse team that featured players from tough backgrounds as well as Bixby Knolls old money. The team also boasted a large contingent of Polynesian players, a hallmark of Poly's for decades.

The music program was becoming a powerhouse, too, drawing students from all over the city who wanted to play for Andy Osman and Chris Stevens. The symphonic orchestra and jazz band performed frequently and took home major awards from festivals around the West Coast.

Academically, PACE and CIC continued to expand and leave their mark, with Greta McGree still running CIC more than twenty years after she founded the academy.

HIGH HONORS

Poly was the toast of the town. California governor Gray Davis came down to celebrate the school in 2000, and the Poly cheerleaders even appeared on Monday Night Football. Legendary coaches like Jerry Jaso, Raul Lara, Don Norford, George Wright and Ron Palmer were all still on campus together. Honors that Ashley could never have imagined continued to pour in. *Sports Illustrated* named Poly America's best high

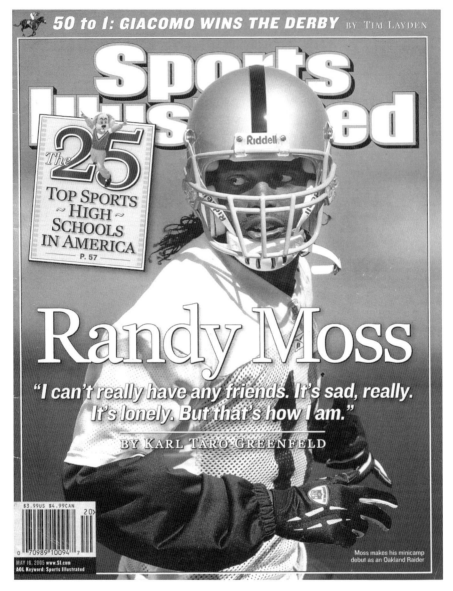

Cover of the 2005 *Sports Illustrated* issue where Poly was honored as America's best high school sports program. *Author archives.*

school sports program in 2005, and ESPN followed suit a few years later. Poly won a California Distinguished School Award as one of the top four schools in the state and was named School of the Century by the California Coaches Association in 2000.

"If I had to pick one thing, probably the *Sports Illustrated*, that probably meant the most," said Ashley. "To see the Jackrabbit on the cover of *Sports Illustrated*, I mean that's a pretty amazing thing. For a public school to get there, and the fact that Poly was really good academically and was getting better all the time was a huge, huge deal to me."

The school's academics were honored as well, as Poly broke the National Merit Scholars record with ten winners in 2002, the same year the school set a new record for most winners of the nationwide NCTE writing contest, the top honor for high school writers. Of the one hundred NCTE winners in 2002, seven were Poly seniors.

US News and World Report ran feature stories on PACE and CIC as the two top public school magnets in the country, lauding both their academic rigor and diversity. The music program was recognized as the best in the nation as well, winning six GRAMMY high school awards including two Signature GRAMMYs, given to the top program in America.

MARCHING INTO THE FUTURE

Ashley stepped down in 2011, and the school hasn't had a long-term principal since. Mel Collins, Gwen Mack and Victor Jarels all served as co-principals with Ashley, with Jarels's ten-year tenure the longest. Joe Carlson, Diane Prince, Quentin Brown and Bill Salas have all served in the posts in the years since Ashley left.

Some things have changed—the auditorium has been retrofitted to survive a strong earthquake. Since it was the only building that wasn't toppled in 1933, it looks like Poly's oldest building will be around for a lot longer. Burcham Field received a turf upgrade and an all-weather track in 2018, with further upgrades planned to the school's historic pool on the way.

Some things, of course, have not changed. Not in the last year, the last decade or the last century. Poly is still a nationally known athletic powerhouse, with young NFL stars like JuJu Smith-Schuster playing on the same field as perennial Pro Bowlers like Jurrell Casey and DeSean Jackson.

The school continues to be an academic force, with more students accepted to the UC system than any other public school.

From a one-room school to a sprawling, historic campus with priceless works of public art and more than four thousand students, it's been quite a journey for Long Beach's first high school. On a given day you might flip on the television and see Billie Jean King receiving the Presidential Medal

Poly's record-setting signing class of 2017, when forty-two students signed college scholarships. *Photo by the authors.*

The diverse Poly student body celebrates another big win for the school's football team in 2018. *Photo by John Napalan, Art O'Neill.*

of Freedom, or you might see Poly alum Keith Kellogg serving as Donald Trump's national security advisor. You might flip past a Snoop Dogg music video or happen upon a TV show featuring Carl Weathers.

These alums as well as the thousands of students who walk through the gates of the school each day represent a special story in America. They represent a school that faced down tremendous odds and emerged victorious. It achieved those victories despite a lack of money and a surplus of obstacles. But because of Poly's incredible history and the pride it's inspired, the school has lived up to those challenges, it's met them and it's created an unparalleled legacy, written in green and gold.

10

JACKRABBIT TRADITIONS

The American high school experience is rooted in tradition, with fight songs, shared customs and even superstitions passed down through the generations. But few schools across the country can compete with Poly's national acclaim, its star-studded list of alumni or its unique cultural significance. In Long Beach specifically, one's identity is often tied to one's alma mater. When two Long Beach natives meet for the first time, a common opening question is "What high school did you go to?" Those who answer "Poly" have formed an immediate bond over 120 years in the making.

The oldest surviving element of the Poly campus is at the heart of the quad, sitting at the base of the school's flagpole. The cornerstone of the original administration building was laid in December 1910, and it was preserved following the Long Beach earthquake in 1933. That cornerstone was moved to the middle of the school's quad and surrounded by ruins of the iconic pillars from the front entrance to campus. An homage to the past doesn't just lie at Poly's center; there's also some history outside the school's gates.

At the front of campus at 1600 Atlantic, you'll find a holdover from Poly's original location. Sitting prominently in a circular flower bed just feet from Poly's front gates is Founder's Rock, which was brought over from the original Eighth and American campus to the school's current location in 1911. In the 1971 yearbook, celebrating the school's seventy-fifth anniversary, the following phrase captured the rock's significance to the school: "Founder's Rock, which will always remain the same, representing an unchanging dedication to learning at a time when the only constant is change."

Founder's Rock in front of the main entrance to campus. The rock has been there for more than a half century. *Photo by Stephen Carr.*

Presently, Founder's Rock features a plaque that was presented by the Key Club in 1958. The top of the plaque makes note of Poly's origins, reading "Established 1895," while the bottom of the plaque offers a more unifying message to every Poly student: "Dedicated to those who have gone forth to serve."

As students filter past Founder's Rock to make their way through the front gate, they walk beneath that same message—the one Billie Jean King looks to for inspiration during her visits back home. "Enter to Learn, Go Forth to Serve" is embedded just above the entryway, reminding students of the implicit responsibility of Poly's students and its graduates. The motto was incorporated into the school during the campus rebuild in 1935. Hugh Davies, the official architect overseeing the reconstruction of Poly's campus, was credited with coining the phrase and including it in the new design.

While that may be Poly's oldest official motto, the one most often associated with the school comes from former principal Neil Phillips, who was at the school from 1955 to 1965. The school's Hall of Fame, located in the second-story walkway between the 300 and 400 buildings, was named in his honor when it was opened in 1967. Principal Walter Newland stated at the time,

The completion of the Hall of Fame facility culminates the efforts of the Classes of the Sixties to enshrine forever in the hearts of Poly students the rich heritage of group and individual excellence in student activity that over the past decades has earned for Long Beach Polytechnic the accolade "Home of Scholars and Champions."

FIRSTS

Because of its age and the innovative philosophy of many of the school's head administrators, Poly is home to several firsts. It was the first school in California with a student government, the first to have a PTA, the first high school to graduate with college-style caps and gowns and the school established one of the first JROTC programs west of the Mississippi. Unconfirmed reports in the school's yearbooks have claimed that the Poly cheerleaders were the first high school cheer team in the state to use pompoms.

Poly's yearbook, the *Caerulea*, was first printed in 1902, and its newspaper, the *High Life*, had its first edition in 1916. Other than the *Press-Telegram*, Long Beach's daily newspaper, they're the two oldest continuously running publications in the city.

HAUNTED POLY

Long Beach Poly's been on the same campus for more than a century, and most of its buildings date back to the 1930s. Any institution with that kind of history is bound to be a magnet for stories about ghosts and other mysteries. Poly doesn't have many famous urban legends, although over the years there have been people who've died on campus.

There is one part of the school that's the subject of whispers and speculation: an extensive labyrinth of tunnels that runs underneath the entire campus. The tunnels have been there since the campus was rebuilt after the 1933 earthquake and served a number of purposes. In addition to storage rooms, there are actually classrooms in the tunnels under Poly and areas for people to shelter in case of the school being bombed. In the late 1930s and early 1940s, that wasn't outside the realm of possibility. Because Long Beach was home to so much of America's naval and air force construction, it was considered a prime target—trees in many of the city's parks were cut down to put in antiaircraft guns.

There are several entrances to the tunnels, including large walk-in doors near the auditorium and natatorium. But there are also hatches all over campus that could be lifted, including in at least one classroom.

The scenery is spooky enough that the school used to hold haunted houses in the tunnels near the auditorium in October, and the drama classes would go down to tell scary stories on Halloween.

OTHER POLY TRADITIONS

Another integral component of a high school's identity is its fight song, which was established at Poly in 1914. Pulling from the school's connection to the Midwest, "Loyalty" was selected as the fight song for Long Beach High School over a century ago. The song uses music from "Illinois Loyalty," which was written in 1906 as the fight song at the University of Illinois. Many of Poly's students during that era were from the Midwest, flooding to the coast from states like Illinois, Iowa and Oklahoma. As the population of Long Beach swelled due to the influx of workers from the Midwest, Long Beach became characterized as the "Iowa of the West." Of course, the lyrics to "Loyalty" were altered to fit with Long Beach High School, but the familiar cry of "Che-he, Che-ha, Che-ha-ha-ha" remained in the middle of the tune.

The Polyettes, the Jackrabbits' historic cheerleading squad, has its own tradition. For decades, they were the largest cheer group in California, according to the *Press-Telegram*. Everyone from actress Cameron Diaz to PACE counselor Connie Loggins has held the green and gold pompoms of the Polyettes. During Poly football games over the years, the Polyettes helped lead the crowd in some classic cheers, asking the green and gold faithful "How funky is your chicken? How loose is your goose?" warning the opposition that "You don't want no Green Machine" and singing the famous rallying cry "So Hard to be a Rabbit."

As the years have gone on, Poly has continued to add more traditions and preserve its history. In the early 1980s, Poly got its logo, the Jackrabbit leaning on an LB, that's been used for almost forty years. It came from a student contest—the winning entry coming from Mauro Quibin, a student at nearby St. Anthony.

In the center of the hallway inside the Phillips Hall of Fame is Poly's school seal, a green circle with a cursive gold *L* inside, adorned with green banners that read "Home of Scholars and Champions."

The first page of the original sheet music for "Loyalty," a Poly fight song written by student Thurlyne Buffum in 1914. *From Poly historical archives.*

While the seal has been there for decades, only recently has an unofficial set of rules been applied to it. It is believed that starting in the mid-'90s, new students were informed during orientation that only seniors and Poly alumni would be permitted to walk on the seal. While the school is unable to enforce such a policy, it has still found ways to uphold and celebrate Poly's history.

CAMPUS UPGRADES

As recently as 2017, when the school's auditorium completed a $24 million renovation project, parts of its original charm were preserved. The original sides of the auditorium seats from 1931 were maintained at the ends of each row, containing an interlocking "PHS" logo and adorned with intricate designs, all in gold.

Inside the auditorium there's a newer annual tradition, the Mr. and Mrs. Jackrabbit pageant, which began in 1994. The event is essentially a full-length talent show for members of the senior class, after which a pair of students are chosen by a panel of judges to be Mr. and Mrs. Jackrabbit, mirroring the more conventional Homecoming King and Queen.

The interior of the school's auditorium was rebuilt in 2017, but the original historic siding to the seats was preserved and restored. *Photo by Stephen Carr.*

The school recently replaced its historic track with a new all-weather surface and knocked down the seventy-five-year-old bleachers to put in a modern facility.

Poly's traditions help tie together the spirit of the school throughout the decades, where third- and fourth-generation Jackrabbits have become commonplace. Long Beach families, especially those in the Eastside neighborhood surrounding the campus, have formed an unwavering pride in the school, affectionately referred to in some circles as the "Funk House." As longtime principal Shawn Ashley told ESPN in a 2009 story about Poly's wide-ranging success: "The feeling in Long Beach is that this is their school, their birthright. Parents went here and they want their kids going here."

11

THE ART MUSEUM ON THE EASTSIDE

While the earthquake of 1933 may have destroyed iconic elements of Poly's original architecture, it also provided an opportunity for a fresh start to the beloved campus. Because the disaster struck during the heart of the Great Depression, Poly's rebuild coincided with an influx of federal spending on public works projects, including initiatives focused on the arts.

Poly's campus was a direct beneficiary of the Works Progress Administration (WPA) and its ambitious Federal Art Project, which began in 1935. The largest arts project contained in FDR's New Deal, the Federal Art Project helped employ thousands of artists across the country, and its impact on Poly's campus has been preserved to this day.

MURALS

Perhaps the most iconic work from this era is a mural that only a select few will get the chance to see up close. Located in a stairwell between the 300 and 400 buildings at the front of Poly's campus, leading up to the Phillips Hall of Fame, *Industrial Activities in Long Beach* now sits behind sealed glass, closed off to everyday foot traffic.

The image of Long Beach's bustling waterfront is an egg tempera painting on plaster, stretching approximately eighteen feet tall and thirty-two feet wide. The mural shows a crowded multiracial array of surfers,

JACKRABBIT SPOTLIGHT: MILDRED BRYANT BROOKS

Accomplished artist Mildred Bryant Brooks attended Long Beach High School in the late 1910s and went on to an award-winning art career for her etchings of trees and landscapes. During the 1930s, she produced several etched landscapes and was described as creating "America's best etchings of trees" by *Los Angeles Times* art critic Arthur Millier.

In 1936, Brooks had her own one-woman show at the Smithsonian Institute in Washington, D.C., and she received twenty-two national and international awards during her career. Her work is featured in collections at the Library of Congress, New York Public Library, Los Angeles County Museum of Art, Dayton Art Institute, University of Nebraska, Cleveland Museum of Art and the Los Angeles Public Library.

sailors, fishermen and even your average Long Beachians enjoying a day at the beach, revealing what days along the waterfront might have looked like during the mid-1930s. While it was a difficult time for most of the country, Long Beach's advantageous location along the Pacific coast helped insulate the city from the full effects of the Depression. The mural depicts some of the primary industries in the thriving port city: fishing, shipping, oil production and the presence of the U.S. Navy's Pacific Fleet. (A color photo of the mural is included in the insert.)

The mural was commissioned with funds from the WPA's Federal Art Project, which is credited in the lower left-hand corner of the painting. The artists—Ivan Bartlett and Jean Swiggett—were both Poly graduates who went on to study at Chouinard Art Institute in Los Angeles and have successful careers in the arts. They also worked together on several other Federal Art Project murals throughout Southern California. The mural at Poly was completed in 1939, and thanks in part to its current glass enclosure, it has remained in impressive condition over the last eighty years.

The other WPA-funded mural on campus is on the second floor of the administration building. The mural is also inaccessible to foot traffic, as it sits behind the clock that faces out to Poly's quad. The painting is titled *High School Students*, and it depicts a group of Poly students engaged in everyday activities on campus.

High School Students, a WPA mural in the administration building, painted in 1939 by Eugene Brooks and preserved in the same location today. *Photo by Stephen Carr.*

FACES ON CAMPUS

The art on Poly's campus isn't just contained to paintings, however. One of the school's unique works is a colorful Catalina tile mural located at the southwest corner of campus at the edge of the 300 building. The mural features a triumphant Mercury soaring above the earth, with a Douglas DC-1 flying below him and a Union Pacific passenger train running across the bottom. Just below the train are the words "Speed Is the Greatest Factor of Modern Life" etched along the base of the mural. (A color photo of the mural is included in the insert.)

While the artist remains unknown, the mural was completed in 1935. The first DC-1 aircraft had been produced in December 1933, and its inclusion in the mural foreshadows Long Beach's sustained connection to aviation over the years.

Another interesting feature of the Poly campus that has been sustained since the 1930s are the somewhat mysterious green faces around campus. Adorning entryways on both floors of the 100 and 200 buildings, these cast concrete relief panels depict not only prominent historical figures but also significant members of the Poly community. There are also some generic faces that pay homage to various industries like architecture, aviation, chemistry and filmmaking.

The faces on are arranged in columns of five, placed on each side of the doorway. One grouping of five, located on the second story of the administration building, brings together the likes of authors Miguel de Cervantes and Mark Twain, Greek mathematician Euclid and two of Poly's finest in David Burcham and Jane Harnett. Over the years, there has been debate over the identities of some of the faces, and the sculptor remains anonymous.

The reconstructed Poly campus of the 1930s was brought forth from natural disaster, which just so happened to coincide with unprecedented federal investment in the arts. That has made the school a time capsule of sorts, showcasing some unique designs of the era. The campus itself was reinvented in the Streamline Moderne architectural style, and in the decades since its construction, Poly has preserved its history and remains a symbol of the Federal Art Project's success in the United States.

Some of the face sculptures that frame the doorways of Poly's major buildings, built as part of the WPA in the 1930s. Faces here include David Burcham, Euclid and Mark Twain. *Photo by Stephen Carr.*

12

POLY AT WAR

Poly has lived through both world wars, which caused challenges that fundamentally reshaped the student body and the campus itself. To this day, there remain tributes and memorials on the Poly campus that preserve the school's link to U.S. war efforts throughout the twentieth century.

WORLD WAR I

The First World War began less than three years after the opening of Poly's current campus, and the United States' involvement in the war followed a few years after that. The United States declared war in April 1917, passing the Selective Service Act the next month to draft nearly three million men from across the country into military service. That mobilization of troops directly impacted the Poly campus, where students and faculty alike were subject to the draft.

Poly students turned soldiers wrote letters back to the school, describing their experiences in Europe. One student, Hugo Hihn, received the French Croix de Guerre for bravery in battle after he and four other soldiers snuck into a forest and captured eight German gunners before marching them to headquarters.

Pete Lenz, a Poly High graduate, described some of the horrors of trench warfare in a letter back to the school. Lenz was a combat engineer who dug trenches in fields so muddy they came up to his hip boots. "All of this was done under gas, and believe me it's some pleasant task wearing a gas mask for several hours. The mask cuts into the flesh, and I sometimes wondered which was worse, the gas or the mask." He had one artillery shell go through his arm and shoulder and another go through his knee, forcing him to spend time in eight different hospitals, but the Salvation Army and Red Cross saved his life.

Nine Poly students were killed in the war, and they were remembered in the 1919 *Caerulea*, which was dedicated to "our crusaders triumphant…who have united a new world of justice, of hope, and of humanity."

JROTC

The war spawned the desire for a more prepared civilian population with some basic military training, should the need for a draft arise in the future. With the National Defense Act of 1916, the Junior Reserve Officers Training Corps (JROTC) was established in the United States. Just three short years later, Charles Boice founded the JROTC program at Long Beach Poly in 1919, making it one of the first JROTC programs west of the Mississippi. Only two other programs in California have been credited with predating Poly's, which has lasted for over a century to become the second-oldest active JROTC in the state.

In 1954, the current JROTC building on campus and the recently demolished bleachers at the adjacent Burcham Field were constructed. What spectators may not have known was that an active rifle range was right below their feet, inside those concrete bleachers. Poly's JROTC students fired .22 rifles and pistols in the eight-lane range, shooting at targets that were cranked across the fifty-foot space in front of a sand backdrop. In the mid-'90s, JROTC programs switched to pellet rifles and reduced the range size to thirty-three feet, all while Poly's on-campus rifle range was still active, according to longtime instructor Johnny Byrum, a retired U.S. Army first sergeant who spent two decades with the Poly JROTC program.

"You represent your family, you represent your community, and you represent Poly High School everywhere you go, and that's what I pushed on the kids in the program," said Byrum, who was at Poly from 1990 to 2010. "When you walk on that campus, you've got to be a winner to go to Poly High School. And if you're not, you sure will be before you leave there."

Poly is one of very few high school campuses to feature what was once an active shooting range for the Jackrabbits JROTC program. The range was located under the bleachers at Burcham Field. *Courtesy* Caerulea *archives.*

WORLD WAR II

While the First World War helped unite and inspire a young Poly campus, the second iteration in the 1940s was a much more complicated matter. The student body once again mobilized in the war efforts following the attack on Pearl Harbor at the end of 1941, as that year's *Caerulea* would describe:

> *With our country at war the need for the defense of our land stirs the heart of every freedom-loving American youth. This year more than ever students are leaving Poly to go directly into vital defense work in our community, into airplane factories, shipyards, and oil refineries. Upon graduation many are joining the Army, Navy and Marines.*

By the next school year, the JROTC membership swelled to over three hundred members, and the program received a federal inspection in May 1943. The Portia Club put together two huge service flags with blue and gold stars, representing Poly alums fighting in the war and those who died in combat.

Poly's campus was also greatly impacted by Japanese internment, which caused a sizable rift on campus. The city of Long Beach, and thus Poly by extension, had a large Japanese American population that essentially vanished during this period. The 1943 graduating class featured no Japanese students, which was an abrupt change from the years prior. Some students on campus even made signs with racist caricatures as part of an effort to raise money for the war. For those familiar with Poly's current reputation for inclusiveness and racial harmony, it's a jarring sight, reflective of the tensions of the era.

As it did a quarter century prior, the school pushed forth efforts to sell war bonds and savings stamps to buy fighter planes, using phrases like "Bomb de bums wid Bunnie Bombers" and "If you can't wear khaki buy a bond, by cracky!"

The student body also grew as the city's population began to increase. An estimated 170,000 workers flocked to Long Beach to build planes, ships and other war machinery. Many Poly students were called to the war prior to graduation—once they turned eighteen, they were off to serve.

As of March 1, 1944, a total of fifty-four Poly alums had been killed in action. They were honored at the *Polycade of Freedom*, a pageant held in the school auditorium that served as a memorial to war heroes. It was organized and designed by students, who wrote a script for the event, read poetry and played music, hoping to "display the story of America's struggle for liberty from the revolutionary war up to present day."

The event helped establish a fund to build the Memorial Library on campus, which would eventually be opened in 1952. To this day, the main foyer of Poly's library has a sign that reads, "We honor the war dead not with wreaths, but works. Not speeches but service. Not praise but peace."

The library isn't the only memorial in the city. Poly and Wilson students wrote home from the war, requesting that the city build a football stadium for its youth so that they'd have something special for after the war was over. Those letters spurred a bond election that passed overwhelmingly, funding the construction of Veterans Memorial Stadium in East Long Beach, where Poly's football team has played its home games for the last sixty years.

Several Poly graduates served honorably in the war and were honored for their accomplishments. Francis Denebrink served in the navy during World War I and went on to become the head of the navigation department at the Naval Academy from 1936 to 1939. He would serve as a rear admiral in World War II, commanding naval forces in the Pacific Fleet as part of America's occupation of Japan. Denebrink was also responsible for the

Schools sold war bonds to help raise money to build bomber planes, many of which were built a few miles away from Poly in Long Beach. The racist caricature on the sign highlights the difference between the 1940s and today. *Courtesy* Caerulea *archives.*

Near the conclusion of World War II, Poly held a memorial in the campus's quad for the alums who'd died fighting overseas. *Courtesy* Caerulea *archives.*

logistic support of the U.S. naval forces in the Korean War and retired as a vice admiral in 1956 after receiving the Army Distinguished Service Medal, three Legions of Merit and the Navy Marine Corps medal in his career.

Brigadier General Gerald A. Counts also served in both world wars, earning the Legion of Merit with the oak-leaf cluster and a Bronze Star for his service during World War II. After his time at Poly and his graduation from West Point in 1917, Counts took graduate courses at MIT and Caltech. Following his service overseas, Counts returned to West Point as an assistant mathematics professor. That began a thirty-four-year career at the Military Academy, which included stints as the head of both the physics and chemistry departments, and a two-year term as dean of the Academic Board. He received numerous awards during his forty-five years of active military service and was the oldest general officer in the army still on active duty upon his retirement in 1959. The Brigadier General Gerald A. Counts Award is given out each year to West Point's top graduate from the physics department.

In the United States Air Force, Major General Edward W. Anderson commanded a number of fighter groups in the United States and England during World War II, earning numerous awards—including a Legion of Merit, Silver Star, Bronze Star and Air Medal—during his thirty years of military service. Even Hugh David Burcham, the son of Poly's longtime principal, served as an active-duty U.S. Navy chaplain during World War II.

In the decades since, Poly has had several distinguished members of the armed forces, including many who have been decorated with Purple Hearts and other major honors. Keith Kellogg, an army lieutenant general, received the Distinguished Service Medal and the Silver Star, among many other honors. Kellogg was President Donald Trump's acting national security advisor in February 2017 and was still serving as Vice President Mike Pence's national security advisor as of this writing.

"GI JO"

One of the most interesting connections between Poly and World War II came from an unlikely source—music played on the battlefield. Poly alumna Jo Stafford was one of the most popular singers in the world during in the 1940s and '50s, especially among U.S. troops. According to her 2008 obituary in the *Los Angeles Times*, "Stafford's solo career began with an inextricable link to the war. A favorite of American soldiers, she was told by a veteran of the Pacific that 'The Japanese used to play your records on loudspeakers across from our foxholes so that we'd get homesick and surrender.'" This earned her the clever nickname "GI Jo" among U.S. soldiers.

However, her influence was not contained just to the battlefield, nor to the confines of the war. Following the Allied victory in 1945, she became a valuable component of the United States' diplomatic efforts across the globe. Beginning in 1950, she was given her own weekly show, called *The Jo Stafford Show*, on Voice of America, which broadcast American-sourced news and entertainment in more than forty languages across the world.

According to a 1951 article in *Collier's Weekly*, her show was broadcast every Wednesday "in which a potential audience of 200,000,000 people in all corners of the earth listens to her sing songs, play records and deliver messages about the advantages of living in a democracy like the United States."

The popularity of American music across the world—and of Stafford specifically—made the program a successful vehicle to speak directly to young people across the globe and deliver a clear message about American democracy. In the decade following World War II, Jo Stafford was a prominent figure in this effort. As a high-ranking State Department official told *Collier's Weekly*, "I hate to admit it, but where 10 foreigners may have heard of Jo Stafford, only one has heard of Warren Austin, our chief delegate of the United Nations. The girl is tremendously important in world diplomacy today."

13

TRAILBLAZING JACKRABBITS IN WOMEN'S SPORTS

Years before the California Interscholastic Federation was established as the state's governing body of high school sports in 1913, Poly was already having tremendous success in athletics. Much of the school's success throughout the years has come from girls' sports. From its early days, Poly afforded its female students an opportunity to compete, and the school has established a pioneering legacy in girls' high school athletics.

The earliest girls' sports team to find championship success at Poly was the basketball program. The girls' basketball team defeated the boys' team in an early 1910s matchup with bragging rights and ice cream on the line. The Jackrabbits won their first of three consecutive state championships in 1907, setting the standard for one of the most successful girls' hoops program in America. That first championship predated Poly's first official girls' CIF title by a whopping sixty-seven years, since girls' sports weren't added by the CIF until 1973, shortly after the passage of Title IX in 1972.

Girls' sports teams at Poly have won a total of twenty-nine CIF championships and twenty-one state titles since 1973, the most of any high school in both categories.

"You've got Billie Jean King, maybe the greatest female athlete ever in terms of what she's done on and off the court," said Mark Tennis, editor of *Cal-Hi Sports* and a California sports historian. "Basketball, volleyball, track—they've all been good. The girls have been at the forefront of sports at Poly. Long Beach is one of the real birthplaces of the women's sports movements. They had athletes like Martha Watson competing and dominating before girls' sports were even sanctioned by Title IX."

G.A.A. CODE

As a member of the Girls' Athletic
  Association,
I will be a good sport at all times;
I will be loyal to my friends and
  school interests;
I will be fair in competition and
  in my judgment of others;
I will be courteous, thoughtful, and
  respectful;
I will be ready to give my
  friendship freely but sincerely;
I will be willing to cooperate
  with the Association;
I will try to face my school duties
  and activities fairly and
  squarely;
I will play up and play the game
  of life.

Top: The state champion Long Beach Poly girls' basketball team of 1908, which competed against other high schools and even colleges in Southern California. *Courtesy* Caerulea *archives.*

Left: The Girls' Athletic Association code; before Title IX's passage, this was the only sports activity available for most local students. *Courtesy* Caerulea *archives.*

JACKRABBIT SPOTLIGHT: MARTHA WATSON

When track and field was added as a sport in the GAA in 1962, junior student Martha Watson made history as one of the Poly "Flyers." That year's yearbook looked back on her unique accomplishment: "[T]he highlight of this successful year of the Girls' Athletic Association was November 29, 1962. On this date Martha Watson broke the national high school record for the long jump." Watson comfortably broke the previous record of 16-08 by jumping 17-01.25 and went on to compete in four Olympic Games for the United States.

Even without formal girls' sports programs on campus, Poly continued to turn out top-notch female athletes, including four-time Olympian Martha Watson, shown here in 1965. *Courtesy Caerulea archives.*

Going back to the early days, "physical training" courses were first offered to girls at Poly in 1911 and taught by Miss Vinnie Gee. A few years later, the Girls' League was started in 1914, representing the first of its kind in California. The Girls' Athletic Association (GAA) was formed in 1921, providing a more formal structure for girls on campus to play sports.

Despite not being able to compete for Poly, the athletes were still able to accomplish great things.

Girls' sports were added in full in the 1975–76 school year, and female athletes began competing in the Moore League. Girls' badminton was the first girls' program to win a league title for Poly.

Things really took off in the 1990s, as Poly's girls' basketball and girls' track programs began dominating the competition. Girls' basketball won its first of six CIF titles in 1995, going on a run a decade later with four championships from 2007 to 2010 and then another in 2017. That run also included four straight CIF State championships from 2006 to 2009, plus two more in 2013 and 2014. Head coach Carl Buggs and his wife and assistant coach, Lakeisha, took the girls' hoops program to among the nation's best and gave Buggs the most state titles in California history.

Poly's legacy as a trailblazing girls' sports powerhouse continues; Poly's 2017 CIF championship girls' basketball team celebrates their win. *Photo by Stephen Dachman.*

Despite legitimate accomplishments by other programs on campus, nobody can compete with the success of the girls' track and field team at Long Beach Poly. The Jackrabbits have won a staggering twenty CIF Championships since 1980 and fifteen state championships since 1992. That's the year when legendary coach Don Norford won his first track title with the Jackrabbits, and he has gone on to be the winningest coach in state history, working with both track programs and the football team at his alma mater. Longtime assistant coach Crystal Irving officially took over as head coach in 2015, promptly continuing the legacy with a CIF title in her first season.

An alum herself, Irving has been the perfect role model for the talented young women of Long Beach Poly, also serving as the first female athletic director in school history.

> *I always tell our girls they have an inner strength that guys don't have. We can do more than guys because of the way we're made and raised as women. We can be mothers, we can run companies, we can mother other children and still we don't break. We can go through adversity, wins, and losses, and not break.*

14

SCHOLARS AND CHAMPIONS AND MUSICIANS

While barrels of ink have been spilled about Poly's athletic and academic programs, the school's music department has a storied history of its own, one celebrated by proud parents who have created ubiquitous "Scholars & Champions & Musicians" merchandise, adding a musical twist to the school's famous motto.

Former Poly musician Kent Hayworth wrote a history of the Poly program that provides an excellent outline of some of the highs and lows of the last century. The music program was founded shortly after the school first opened by George C. Moore, with the church that housed the school also serving as its first rehearsal and performance space.

"The original orchestra was just a few players and lacked complete instrumentation," wrote Hayworth. "From this humble beginning would grow a legend in music education. It is worth noting that the Poly music department is the oldest musical organization in Long Beach." As the school grew and moved to its own campus, the music program grew in concert. An influx of midwestern students had a major impact on the kinds of music selected for performance, with "Illinois Loyalty" serving as the basis of the school's fight song.

In 1931, Anthony Gill was hired as music director, a role he would serve in for twenty-five years, teaching music in tents on Burcham Field after the earthquake until the auditorium was rebuilt. In the mid-1940s, the school finally got its own music room; until then, all the music classes were conducted in the auditorium.

Above: Poly's 1926 band, which won several regional and state-wide awards. *Courtesy* Caerulea *archives.*

Left: The first of many major awards won by Poly's music programs, this banner hangs in the school's Hall of Fame walkway. *Photo by Stephen Carr.*

During World War II, Poly musicians were a big part of the school's sizable war efforts, holding a charity concert drive that helped fund the construction of a B-17 bomber that went off to the Pacific with a Jackrabbit painted on its side. When Long Beach soldiers flew home after the war's end, the Poly band was there to greet them at the airport.

The Poly music program continued to grow throughout the postwar boom, and there are cabinets full of trophies and awards from that period around campus. In 1958, Robert Dill took over as music director, a role he'd serve in for sixteen years.

Dill forged an alliance with the JROTC that ended up as the foundation for Poly's much-lauded jazz ensembles. Students were required to take a PE class, and since JROTC was considered a class of that category, the JROTC Band class effectively snuck another music class into the curriculum.

The Poly jazz ensemble participated in the Hollywood Bowl Battle of the Bands in the 1960s and has remained an acclaimed group on campus. In 1976, Poly set a record that still stands by putting six alums in that year's Walt Disney All-American College Band, an annual collection of the top forty musicians in the country.

In the late '70s and early '80s, cuts in funding as well as on-campus issues led to the music program falling into disarray. That was until Carl Cohn went to a UCLA teacher's information day looking to hire a new music director for Poly in 1982, someone who was young and energetic and willing to work with a diverse population at a school that was regaining its place of prominence.

One of his interviews was with Andy Osman, a Whittier native whose dream was not to be a musician, but a music teacher. "Carl introduced himself and said, and this is a quote, 'The music department at Poly is dismal,'" remembered Osman with a laugh. "I had never heard of Poly, but they were looking for a music teacher. They offered me the job—I was young and energetic and looking for any kind of high school gig."

Osman came on campus in the fall of 1983 and was at Poly for more than thirty-five years, the longest-tenured music head in school history. After visiting nearby middle schools, Osman knew that, at the very least, there would be big numbers in the Poly music program. He quickly began increasing the enrollment, and the school responded by adding music classes.

"I did not fully realize what the population of the school was like, the mixture of neighborhood kids and PACE and CIC kids, it was kind of just blind luck," said Osman.

By the end of the '80s, Poly was invited to the state music conference, and in 1989 the Poly orchestra backed award-winning alum Marilyn Horne in a famous concert at the First Congregational Church, a fundraiser that purchased the acoustic shell the school has used ever since.

"That was a real watershed moment in letting the community know something good was happening here," said Osman.

The Poly music program took its next step in 1996, with the abrupt departure mid-semester of the school's band instructor. Chris Stevens had never taught before and didn't have a teaching credential, but he was given a shot as a long-term substitute with an emergency credential for the rest of the year.

Stevens, who was a jazz musician, liked teaching, and Osman gave him a brief interview while the pair watched a Kings hockey game at Stevens's house that summer.

"He had been at Poly for twelve years at that point and he said, 'This job is not a stepping stone to me,'" recalled Stevens. "Straight up. He'd already put in place the foundation of the program. I'm grateful to him daily for providing that foundation."

Stevens began expanding Poly's jazz program and oversaw the rapidly improving marching band, while Osman grew the instrumental orchestra. Longtime piano teacher Julia Gustafson was on staff as well, and she added lower-level orchestra to her teaching load when demand required it. With that experienced trio, Poly has been in the rare position as a public school of having three music instructors with several decades of tenure.

The school has since won numerous awards, including six GRAMMYs, for being among the finest schools in the nation, with two Signature Gold GRAMMY awards for being the best, both of which came with actual GRAMMY trophies.

"I'm not a trophy guy," said Osman. "But the GRAMMYs are pretty cool. You feel really good about that."

Osman has won awards himself, including a 2010 prize for being the best music educator in Southern California, but he doesn't display those accolades or enjoy talking about them. "I really don't like using awards or trophies as a measure of success," he said. "It's about the performance, about the people in the audience."

That being said, the shelves in the Poly music room are packed with awards. The Poly jazz bands have been consistent winners at the Reno Jazz Festival, the best competition for high school jazz programs in the western United States, with twelve consecutive years placing in the top five, including a win

Chris Stevens, Andy Osman and Julia Gustafson, the teachers who've been running Poly's music programs for decades and have brought them to national prominence. *Photo by Stephen Carr.*

in 2016. Poly's marching band has consistently been in the championship rounds of the biggest competitions in Southern California, and the school's vocal ensembles have been hits as well.

Over the last three decades, Poly students have been able to play just about any instrument they want at the school or sing just about any kind of music. Poly has had a full range of orchestras and bands, with as many as five classes of just jazz band offered at one time. On the vocal side, the school has had formal choirs, gospel choirs and jazz.

"I wasn't aware of the community here, and when it started dawning on me what this school is, the uniqueness of it, I quickly realized I fell into the top job I could ever have dreamed of," said Stevens. "Once I realized the opportunity here and the quality of kid that comes here, there was no reason to leave."

Osman said that other than turning down an offer from Pasadena High just two years into his tenure, he hasn't been tempted to leave Poly either because it's been such a rewarding experience.

"The diversity of this place, the openness, the tolerance, that makes it special," he said. "Part of the power of the school is that it's okay to be an academic geek on this campus, it's okay to be an athlete on this campus and it's okay to be a musician on this campus."

The Poly marching band performing in a parade at Disneyland in 1998–99. *Courtesy* Caerulea *archives.*

A RARE DEDICATION

Shortly before publication of this book, Osman stepped down from his record-setting tenure after being diagnosed with advanced pancreatic cancer. The Poly music community jumped into action and sent Osman into retirement with a rare honor, as the school's auditorium—its oldest building—is now named the Andy Osman Performing Arts Center. Despite the many famous names to come from the school, very few buildings or spaces are named after individuals—Osman's rare dedication to the school earned him the rare dedication in return.

The naming ceremony was attended by hundreds and was covered by publications ranging from the *LA Times* to NPR, which featured Osman on its popular radio show *All Things Considered*. At the dedication, Osman said,

> *I can't tell you how much I appreciate the support, thoughts and prayers. This honor is beyond anything one can imagine.*
>
> *In these past two months, I've had the incredible good fortune to hear from many students and alums. I can't tell you how meaningful that is to me. Those notes, those letters, emails, from students, both past and current. They mean more to me than I could ever possibly say.*

15

RAPPERS, SINGERS AND ROCK STARS

Long Beach Poly's musical alums have won at least seven Grammys and recorded dozens of gold and platinum records. The long list of big-name music stars begins with Calvin Cordozar Broadus Jr., better known as Snoop Dogg. The rapper, actor, record producer, television personality and entrepreneur has been outward with his love for the green and gold, often speaking fondly of his time as a Jackrabbit. He attended Poly in the late '80s, and his time at the school is where he first began to discover his talents as a rapper.

"When I rapped in the hallways at school, I would draw such a big crowd that the principal would think there was a fight going on," Snoop told the *Los Angeles Times* back in 1993. "It made me begin to realize that I had a gift. I could tell that my raps interested people and that made me interested in myself."

Now considered an icon in the West Coast rap scene, Snoop helped put Long Beach on the map with the release of his 1993 album *Doggystyle*, which has sold over eleven million copies worldwide.

The music video for his debut single, "Who Am I (What's My Name?)," was filmed on the roof of the legendary VIP Records store, which sits just a few yards from Poly's campus. VIP Records is credited as the birthplace of the G-Funk sound in hip hop, giving a start to local artists like Snoop, Warren G, Nate Dogg, Twinz, The Dove Shack, Tha Eastsidaz and others. Snoop has maintained his ties to Long Beach and is a frequent visitor to Poly football games, even donating jerseys and cleats back to

A young Snoop Dogg—then known as Calvin Broadus—as a sophomore at Poly in 1987. *Courtesy* Caerulea *archives.*

the program. He also returned to Poly for a photo shoot that captured the cover art to his 2008 album, *Ego Trippin'*, posing on Jackrabbit Lane in a Poly letterman jacket.

Snoop has sold over thirty-five million albums worldwide and has become ubiquitous in popular culture, starring in movies, television shows, commercials, video games and just about any other medium imaginable. In an effort to give back to his community, Snoop founded the Snoop Youth Football League in 2005 as a nonprofit youth football league for inner-city children across California.

Nate Dogg attended Poly with Snoop and, along with Warren G, formed the rap group 213, named after Long Beach's area code at the time. Though Warren didn't attend Poly, he has been a fixture in the community and still regularly attends Poly sporting events. In a 2004 *Vice* article, Nate referred to Poly High as the starting point of the group. "This is where 213 was born," he said.

Nate's career was primarily defined as a featured artist, providing hooks for some of the biggest hip hop records of the '90s and 2000s, including "Regulate" with Warren G, "The Next Episode" by Dr. Dre, "Area Codes" by Ludacris and the Billboard No. 1 hit "21 Questions" by 50 Cent. Nate passed in 2011 after complications from multiple strokes, but he left a legacy as hip hop's preeminent vocalist.

But the musical success at Poly isn't just contained to hip hop; nor does it begin or end with Snoop's superstar career. Poly is also home to several other bona fide musical stars and GRAMMY award winners. Spike Jones was Poly's

Kelvin Anderson's V.I.P. Records, across the street from Poly, helped launch the careers of Snoop Dogg and other Long Beach rappers and served as a vital West Coast hub for the rapidly exploding genre. *Photo by Stephen Carr.*

first star on the soundwaves, famous for making satirical covers of popular songs in the 1940s and '50s. Jones scored a number one single in 1948 with his comedic holiday song "All I Want for Christmas Is My Two Front Teeth" and also had his own radio show and television shows on NBC. He would receive two stars on the Hollywood Walk of Fame for his work in music recording and radio.

Pop singer Jo Stafford was one of the most popular singers of her era, and she had a trailblazing career that began during her time at Poly. She was a founding member of a singing group called the Stafford Sisters, making her first radio appearance at age sixteen. Stafford was actually on stage at Poly's newly constructed auditorium when the 1933 earthquake hit, rehearsing for the lead in the school musical that year: Victor Herbert's *Sweethearts*. As she told the *Pittsburgh Post-Gazette* in 1964, "It was a bad quake. The whole school fell down."

Stafford would go on to a groundbreaking career in music, with worldwide fame, four No. 1 records on the Billboard Hot 100, millions of records sold and even a GRAMMY award. As a member of a group called the Pied Pipers, she provided background vocals for Frank Sinatra on the hit song "I'll Never Smile Again" by Tommy Dorsey and His Orchestra. That single was number one on the first ever National Best Selling Retail Records chart on July 27, 1940, Billboard's first tracking of popular music based on nationwide retail record sales.

In 1944, Stafford became the first solo artist signed to Capitol Records, and she had fifty-nine Top-20 charted singles from 1944 to 1955. Stafford's solo career hit new heights in 1952, with the release of the No. 1 hit, "You Belong to Me." That song also reached No. 1 in the United Kingdom, making her the first female artist from any nation to top the UK Singles Chart. By 1954, she had sold over twenty-five million records in her career.

Along with husband Paul Weston, in character and under the pseudonyms Jonathan and Darlene Edwards, Stafford released an album titled *Jonathan and Darlene Edwards in Paris*, which won the 1960 GRAMMY award for Best Comedy Album (musical comedy). (See chapter 12 for more on Stafford's career.)

Speaking of GRAMMYS, mezzo-soprano singer Marilyn Horne was a four-time winner and fifteen-time nominee in her illustrious career. She earned her first award in 1964, then won again in 1973, 1981 and 1993. In 1992, Horne was also awarded the National Medal of Arts, which is the highest honor given to artists by the United States government.

She also received the Kennedy Center Honors in 1995 to recognize her lifetime of contribution to the performing arts. The Kennedy Center described her career thus: "Marilyn Horne has conquered virtually every major opera house in every corner of the repertory, bringing to all of them a vibrant sensitivity, beauty, and sheer magnetism that remain unsurpassed in our time." *Opera News* once referred to Horne as "probably the best singer in the world."

Her career is still celebrated at the Marilyn Horne Museum and Exhibit Center, located at 2 Marilyn Horne Way at the University of Pittsburgh at Bradford. The museum opened on May 6, 2017, in her birthplace of Bradford, Pennsylvania, and features musical recordings, interviews, interactive exhibits and an exclusive documentary film about her career.

Even the world-famous Motown Records featured Long Beach Poly representation. Thelma Houston had an expansive singing career that touched an array of genres, including R&B, soul, gospel, disco and Motown. She released her debut solo album in 1969 and would sign to Motown Records just two years later. She reached the peak of her fame early in 1977 with her chart-topping hit, "Don't Leave Me This Way." The record reached No. 1 on the soul chart, disco chart and the Billboard Hot 100. In addition to

JACKRABBIT SPOTLIGHT: JENNI RIVERA

Janney Rivera would go on to achieve international stardom as Jenni Rivera before her tragic death in 2012. *Courtesy* Caerulea *archives.*

Latin singer and Long Beach native Jenni Rivera went on from Poly to become the highest-selling banda singer ever, with over twenty million records sold worldwide. Rivera released over twenty albums during her award-winning career, which was tragically cut short on December 9, 2012, when she died in a plane crash in Mexico.

Following her death, she received several posthumous honors, including an exhibit at the GRAMMY Museum in Los Angeles, which was the first such exhibit dedicated to a Latin American artist. Locally, Rivera was remembered with the dedication of Jenni Rivera Memorial Park just over a mile from the Poly campus, featuring a 125-foot mural of the iconic singer. The proposal was made by Sixth District councilmember and fellow Poly alum Dee Andrews, and it passed with unanimous approval. At the dedication, Long Beach mayor Robert Garcia stated, "Jenni Rivera was a true Long Beach legend. Her music, and her many philanthropic contributions, touched so many people in our city and around the world. Naming this park after Jenni honors the legacy of one of our city's most inspiring native daughters."

Rivera was just approaching the peak of her fame at the time of her passing. Already a star among the Mexican music community, she was set for a breakout acting role in the mainstream. Just four days before her tragic death, *Deadline* reported that ABC had begun development on a family comedy show called *Jenni*, with Rivera as the star. Unfortunately, the world never got to see her as she was billed to be in the show: "as a strong, middle-class, single Latina woman working to raise a family."

Recognizing her community and charity work, the Los Angeles City Council offered an official proclamation naming August 6 "Jenni Rivera Day."

Rivera's autobiography, *Unbreakable: My Story, My Way*, was released on her birthday following her death and became a

New York Times bestseller in 2013. After that project's success, Telemundo created a television series to tell her life story, which premiered in 2017. The show, titled *Mariposa de Barrio*, shares the title with one of Rivera's songs and translates to "Neighborhood Butterfly."

the track's commercial success, Houston was also awarded Best Female R&B Vocal Performance at the twentieth GRAMMY Awards in 1978.

Rockstar Lita Ford was born in London but moved to Long Beach as a kid and wound up at Poly after originally attending nearby Lakewood High School. At age sixteen, Ford joined the rock band the Runaways, where she was the lead guitarist alongside lead singer Joan Jett. As Ford told *Glide* magazine in 2012, she actually missed her graduation at Poly because she was on tour with the Ramones at the time. After her time with the Runaways, Ford went on to a successful solo career, releasing eight albums following her debut in 1983.

SUBLIME AND OTHERS

Plenty of music fans and Long Beach residents have heard of Sublime, the legendary ska/reggae/punk band from the city fronted by singer-songwriter Bradley Nowell, who tragically died just as the band was blossoming into national prominence. Sublime produced two platinum albums, both of which are littered with references to Long Beach and the city's culture, including "Doin' Time," "What I Got" and "April 29, 1992," which was about the Rodney King riots in Long Beach and around Southern California.

All three of those cuts came from Sublime's self-titled album, released in 1996, a smash hit that went five times platinum.

What many music fans in Long Beach don't know is that Nowell, a Belmont Shore native who attended Wilson High, is also an alum of Poly, a fact his father, Jim, brought to light in an interview with *OC Weekly*. Brad was a CIC student, and he spent half his school days at Poly, attending magnet classes in the morning then busing back to Wilson for afternoon school.

"He always enjoyed the diversity of the Poly student body," Jim confirmed to the authors. "He said it helped him with his songwriting."

JACKRABBIT SPOTLIGHT: HAROLD BROWN

Harold Brown's mother went into labor while riding on the Jackrabbit Coaster at the Pike in 1946 and gave birth to a man who's been racing through life ever since. Harold grew up at Twenty-First and Lemon, in a multicultural society that would inform his musical sensibility as he rose to national fame as part of the band War.

"The Fukuharas had just got out of the concentration camps, we had Samoans, Filipinos, white people, the closest black family was a whole half block away," said Brown. "Way before MLK was marching, I would go stay with Bill Shibley's family and they would come stay at my house—white kids and black kids were already mixing it up in Long Beach."

Brown's love of music was sparked by all the live tunes he heard around the Poly neighborhood growing up, music pouring out of churches and bars and radios. With a drum kit he bought at Morey's Music, Brown sought to join in that tradition. In the summers, he and his neighborhood friends would sit in the Poly bleachers and get a drum circle going. When he arrived at the school, he ran track and played music. Not long after he graduated high school in 1964, he was a professional musician, and he and fellow Poly grad Charles Miller were touring the world with War, their wildly successful '70s funk band, which produced nine gold records and two platinum hits. Long Beach music fans loved having a local group go big—War's album *All Day Music* featured a group shot of the band in front of a grocery store around the corner from Poly.

"Poly was a special place, and I never felt out of place there," he said. "It taught all of us how to be multiculturalistic, if there is such a word."

Poly activities director Vincent Puth remembers seeing Nowell and the rest of the Sublime crew filming homemade music videos in the Poly neighborhood, decked out in green and gold gear.

Few writers captured as many different aspects of the Poly culture as Nowell did, with obvious influences of hip-hop, reggae, funk, punk and even banda music in his songs.

Ikey Owens is another Long Beach native who had great success in the music business. The keyboardist began his career as a member of the Long Beach Dub All-Stars and went on to win a GRAMMY in 2009 as a member of The Mars Volta. Owens was also the keyboardist for Jack White but died tragically in 2014 after suffering a heart attack while on tour.

Other well-known bands have had members with roots at Long Beach Poly, including Dan Regan and Tavis Werts of Reel Big Fish.

While not as famous as the frontmen and women to have graduated from the school, Owens is one of several successful instrumentalists to have come from Poly, including Poly campus security officer and assistant football coach AJ Luke, who has toured as a bassist with several big acts, including Coolio and Snoop Dogg.

The school itself has been name-dropped numerous times in rap verses by artists such as KXNG Crooked, Vince Staples and Tyga and has been the direct subject of songs as well. Snoop Dogg released a song reminiscing about his high school days titled "Too High (Poly High)," featuring fellow Jackrabbits Twinz and Daz Dillinger. Snoop dropped another Poly-themed track with Twinz and Lil ½ Dead in 2009, titled "Green & Gold." The chorus of that track pays homage to the school and the neighborhood it represents: "Green & gold together, lose to y'all never/This Eastside forever, Long Beach Poly."

Other up-and-coming rappers continue to show off their Poly roots, including P-Nice, whose music video "I'm From Long Beach" was filmed in and around the campus; Saviii 3rd, who filmed a music video at the Poly Apartments, the low-income housing complex next to the campus; and HeyDeon, who frequently boasts about his Eastside origins in his lyrics.

Across the generations, former Jackrabbits have found success as singers, rappers, musicians and more. Whether in traditional pop music, Motown, hard rock, hip hop, banda or even comedic satire, Poly has consistently produced a wealth of world-class musicians.

16

FRATERNITIES AND SORORITIES AT POLY

A consistent undercurrent at Poly has been the presence of college-style fraternities and sororities on campus, both in an official and unofficial capacity. The Comus fraternity was founded at Poly in 1909, pioneering a group of exclusive clubs that have experienced varying degrees of influence at the school.

In 1913, the Scarab Architectural Club was formed, and by 1914 the Portia Club had started as well. Both organizations have been longtime sororities on campus, but these groups have each experienced a somewhat turbulent lifespan at Poly. They weren't always welcome and had to deal with government oversight that prevented groups with exclusive membership from existing on campus, along with fellow students resisting their influence.

In 1917, Poly's school newspaper, the *High Life*, detailed a pushback against these groups in an attempt to eradicate them from the campus:

> *One of the most democratic things the paper has done this year has been the consistent effort on its part to rid the school of secret organizations. When there is a law being broken, it is the duty of a newspaper to use its influence to secure the enforcement of this law.* High Life *has done its best in expressing the thoughts of the majority of the students and in ridding the high school of cliques combined to "run the school." If the paper keeps the high ideal of democracy with which it has been started, our Alma Mater will be conspicuous as a school without Frats.*

Comus was one of a dozen of burgeoning on-campus fraternities in the 1950s; this is the 1955 group. *Courtesy* Caerulea *archives.*

Because of this resistance, the fraternities and sororities were forced to create a tongue-in-cheek identity for themselves to maintain a presence on campus. During the 1921–22 school year, the Scarab Club was re-founded under the guise of a zoology club, stating that its purpose was "to further the study of zoology and to create added interest in the subject among the students of the high school." The members wore a pin in the shape of a beetle during their time on campus.

In 1923, the Scarabs hosted a "heart-thrilling Valentine party," which could easily be traced through the generations to the long-running Sweethearts Dance that's still held off-campus every year.

The jabs between these groups and the powers that be continued over the years, with the *High Life* reiterating its efforts to aid the state government in shutting down high school fraternities in 1924. Just two years later, Scarabs boasted about a Christmas party they threw "to prove that they were not devoted entirely to the study of bugs."

By the 1950s, the climate had shifted, and fraternities and sororities were more welcome on campus, becoming an integral part of the Poly experience. Each had their own pins to wear around campus, and they were officially recognized by the school during this period. In 1955 came the debut of the *Caerulea* Tricycle Race, which pitted members of each fraternity against one another in a light-hearted battle for bragging rights. The tricycle race would grow into a famous part of campus culture and an event for students to look forward to each year.

This was the golden era for fraternities and sororities at Poly, with eighteen such groups on campus in 1955 featuring booming membership. Billie Jean

King, class of 1961, was a member of the Zayn sorority during her time at Poly and enjoyed doing volunteer work as part of the club's service mission.

Don Wallace, a Poly alum, said that it was known that the fraternities and sororities ran the student activities and clubs and largely controlled the social life on campus. Wallace was a third-generation Poly student and said that influence was a constant when his grandparents were there in the early twentieth century.

"I think it's like how England has this monarchy," he said. "Even though you resent that you're paying their bills, you still admire the dramatic possibilities."

But things changed for fraternities and sororities in the early 1960s as the State of California banned the use of public funding on groups that had exclusive membership. This move did not get rid of the fraternities and sororities at Poly but did force them to reorganize off-campus, outside of school and district oversight.

Ed Eveland, who was Poly's principal from 1975 to 1979 and had been principal at three Long Beach high schools, didn't exactly agree with the decision to effectively ban the groups from official recognition on the campus. As he told the *Los Angeles Times* in 1987, "The majority of the clubs were very much interested in service to their school," Eveland said. "It's a shame that we were forced [to bar the clubs]."

By the early 1990s, fraternities and sororities had become more prevalent on campus again, with Comus and Sphinx the main fraternities and Scarabs, Zayn and Portia the primary sororities. The membership of these

One Poly sorority that dates back a century is the Scarabs, seen here in the 1955 yearbook. *Courtesy* Caerulea *archives.*

groups has also evolved to reflect the increased diversity of the campus as a whole. The fraternities and sororities at Poly started out as collections of predominantly white students, but they've grown to include members of all ethnic backgrounds while still maintaining some of the same traditions from years past. While their activities have not always been embraced by the school or affiliated with Poly, their influence is ongoing, and for many Poly alums, fraternities and sororities were an integral component of a unique high school experience.

17

PAAL

One of the unique facets of Poly is that it actually has a second, satellite campus. In the fall of 1996, with enrollment on the rise and limited space available on Poly's campus, the school needed a plan to accommodate its students.

"We had a growth problem," admitted former principal HJ Green, who became an assistant superintendent in 1995. "The schools were getting bigger and bigger."

Green worked with his former co-principals, Maggie Webster and Karen Hilburn, to come up with an idea. The original plan was to have an off-site freshman academy just for ninth-grade students, but that presented some major issues. With Poly's thriving magnet programs on campus, many freshmen were taking advanced classes that wouldn't be available on an auxiliary campus.

"The school, through the leadership of Maggie and Karen, came up with the idea of PAAL," Green recalled. "It made a lot of sense and I think it turned out to be, at least to my knowledge, a real asset."

PAAL, or the Poly Academy of Accelerated Learning, opened at the corner of Sixteenth Street and Long Beach Boulevard, less than a half mile down the street from Poly's campus at 1600 Atlantic. The idea behind the additional academy was to provide an opportunity for students who were falling behind to catch up on their schoolwork.

Because of this, PAAL become an upper-division academy at the school, providing educational opportunities exclusively for Long Beach Unified

School District students who had previously been enrolled in tenth or eleventh grade. It also gave students a chance to graduate early, by offering year-long classes that could be taken in a single semester. Students took four ninety-minute classes that met every day, and teachers had scheduled conference periods so they could assist students as needed. While other high schools could only offer sixty credits per semester, PAAL was able to offer its students upward of eighty credits per school year thanks to its unique format. That gave students who needed to graduate early or who needed to catch up a way of doing so.

Despite having their own campus, PAAL students still have the ability to compete for Poly's athletic teams and participate in extracurricular activities on campus. By PAAL's third year, Poly's total enrollment neared five thousand students, with four hundred of those students enrolled at PAAL.

In Poly's WASC Report in March 2001, the school offered the following description of PAAL among the school's areas of strength: "The PAAL campus is a supportive and nurturing environment focusing on success for 11th and 12th graders."

18

HOLLYWOOD POLY

The city of Long Beach lies just twenty-five miles south of Los Angeles, and its proximity to the Entertainment Capital of the World has given Poly direct access to the Hollywood spotlight in a number of ways.

The school has produced a long line of successful actors and actresses throughout its history, and through their contributions in motion pictures, television, radio and music, former Poly students have combined to receive a total of fourteen stars on the Hollywood Walk of Fame.

The early days of Poly's stage productions were put on by the Masque and Sandal Club, which performed plays and musicals inside Poly's auditorium. Dating back to 1917, Poly's annual Christmas concert and pageant was one of the biggest events on campus each year. Many of the prominent actors and actresses who came through Poly got their start in school productions, and famous musician Jo Stafford was in the middle of rehearsal for a musical when the 1933 earthquake hit.

The modern-day theater arts department at Poly has its own classroom and theater along Jackrabbit Lane, dubbed the "Poly Playhouse," and produces a pair of plays and/or musicals each school year. The school also has its own improv comedy team, the Polyesters, which competes against other schools across Southern California and puts on a performance for classmates during the annual Intercultural Fair.

The Poly Drama club puts on "Polywood"; the club has been performing plays and musicals for over a century. *Courtesy* Caerulea *archives.*

EARLY STARS

Though he wasn't actually a graduate of Long Beach Poly, Marion Morrison, better known by his stage name John Wayne, briefly attended the school after his family moved to Southern California from Iowa. Aside from Wayne's brief cameo at Poly, there was another Academy Award–winning actor who attended Poly in the 1920s. Van Heflin was born in Oklahoma before moving to Long Beach, and he went on to a successful career in movies, television and radio spanning from 1936 to 1971. His breakout role came in the 1941 film *Johnny Eager*, when Heflin received the Academy Award for

Best Supporting Actor for his performance as Jeff Hartnett. He also starred in classic films like *The Three Musketeers, Shane* and *3:10 to Yuma.*

Actress Barbara Britton started her career on the stage while she was still a student at Poly and would go on to a career on screen that lasted nearly four decades from 1941 to 1980. Signed to Paramount Pictures in her early twenties, Britton starred opposite some of Hollywood's biggest stars, such as Bob Hope, Gene Autry and even John Wayne. She starred in over thirty motion pictures and more than a dozen television shows in the 1940s and '50s and was a longtime spokesperson for Revlon. A 1949 article in Long Beach's *Independent Press-Telegram* stated, "Today, Barbara Britton's picture has appeared on more national magazine covers than any other motion picture actress in the world."

The year prior, Britton received a key to the City of Long Beach and even had a street named in her honor—Britton Drive in East Long Beach, which runs in front of Minnie Gant Elementary School near Long Beach State University. In 1952, Britton was named the second-ever mayor of Hollywood—an honorary position given to celebs by the Hollywood Chamber of Commerce to promote and emcee important events in the city. She predated show business icons like Betty White, Charlton Heston and Monty Hall in that role, and in 1960, Britton was awarded a star on the Hollywood Walk of Fame for her work in television.

During the same era, actress Laraine Day found success in movies and on the stage and even hosted her own television show called *The Laraine Day Show* in 1951. She appeared in over forty feature films and more than thirty-five television shows and was nicknamed "The First Lady of Baseball" after her marriage to Hall of Fame player, coach and manager Leo Durocher in 1947.

BROADCASTERS

Poly's Hollywood connection extends to the news business as well, where 1939 alumna Ruth Ashton Taylor enjoyed a fifty-year career as a newscaster on radio and television. After starting as a writer and producer working at CBS radio with Edward R. Murrow, she became the first woman on the West Coast to appear on television news when she joined CBS's Los Angeles affiliate in 1951.

She interviewed everyone from Albert Einstein to Jimmy Carter and received a pair of Emmy Awards during her career, including one for lifetime achievement. Called "one of the best newspeople in television" by the *Los Angeles Times*, Taylor was given the Governor's Award for Lifetime Achievement by the Academy of Television Arts and Sciences and received her star on the Hollywood Walk of Fame in 1990.

Joanne Ishimine graduated Poly in the late 1960s and then went to UCLA, beginning a broadcasting career that took her behind the desk at ABC for twenty years. Ishimine, who is of Japanese descent, produced and narrated a documentary on Japanese internment for ABC.

RECENT CELEBS

More recently, stars like Cameron Diaz and Carl Weathers have emerged on the big screen. Weathers was a member of the Poly football team, graduating from Poly in 1966, and went on to a brief career in the NFL with the Oakland Raiders. As an actor, Weathers appeared in over thirty films and is best known for his role as Apollo Creed in the *Rocky* movie franchise, along with his roles in *Predator* and *Happy Gilmore*. He also worked on twenty television shows and even played himself in the hit comedy series *Arrested Development*.

Though she was only at Poly for a short time, Long Beach native Tiffani-Amber Thiessen was a member of the CIC program on campus. Her star emerged quickly in the '90s thanks her memorable TV roles as Kelly Kapowski on *Saved by the Bell* and as Valerie Malone on *Beverly Hills, 90210*.

Carl Weathers—E

A standout football player who went to the NFL, Carl Weathers is better known now for his work as an actor. *Courtesy* Caerulea *archives*.

Other notable actors include silent film actress Edna Tichenor, who appeared in several films in the 1920s, and Percy Daggs III, who has appeared in fifteen television series, including a leading role in *Veronica Mars*. Perry Mattfeld, a more recent Poly alum, had recurring roles on *Shameless* and *Wizards of Waverly Place* and is starring in a new series on the CW, *In the Dark*. Outside of scripted television, Poly alumna Seinne Fleming was one of the standout contestants on the 2018 season of *The Bachelor*. A member of Poly's class of 2008 who also graduated from Yale University, Fleming was lauded for speaking openly on the show about how black women are portrayed in popular culture. She also made numerous appearances on the subsequent season of *The Bachelorette*.

JACKRABBIT SPOTLIGHT: CAMERON DIAZ

Diaz began a modeling career at age sixteen while she was a student at Poly but quickly found success on the big screen. In 1994, she debuted alongside Jim Carrey in *The Mask* and went on to star in nearly fifty films, including *There's Something About Mary*, *Any Given Sunday*, *Charlie's Angels* and the *Shrek* franchise. Somewhat ironically, she also starred in *Being John Malkovich*, which was the directorial debut of director Spike Jonze, who got his nickname from famous band leader and Poly grad Spike Jones.

Diaz's story is a perfect Poly story. She grew up in the Wrigley, just three blocks from where Billie Jean King's parents lived. Diaz's father, Emilio, was Cuban American and worked for an oil company. Diaz's house had a waste duct at the end of the street (which has since been turned into a dog park).

"We had eighteen wheelers driving down the front of my house all day long," she said.

Diaz attended Los Cerritos and Hughes in affluent Bixby Knolls for elementary and middle school, not because they were her neighborhood schools but because she was an ethnic minority, which gave the schools a financial incentive.

"We didn't have to bus in because we could walk over the railroad tracks," she said. "We would walk over the tracks and under the freeway to get to Los Cerritos, a place that only accepted us because they were paid to. And they weren't Blue Line railroad tracks, they were harbor lines from the Port, so we were dodging full on trains with huge containers."

Diaz was blond-haired and blue-eyed, and it left her feeling between worlds, not fully accepted by Hispanic students or white students at school. "I had a lot of identity struggles as a child because I was not white, and I didn't consider myself white," she said.

When she arrived at Poly in the late 1980s, the environment was the exact opposite. Racial minorities were the majority, but there was a diversity of ethnicities and socioeconomic backgrounds.

"I learned how to connect with people who were of different cultures and mindsets and religions because I had that experience in the microcosm of the Poly quad," she said. "Being able to go to each group and have conversations relative to the people there, I felt like I was able to go into the world a little bit better. That to me is one of the great educations of Poly as much as anything else is that diversity."

Diaz did a semester of drama and a semester of Polyettes cheerleading her freshman year, which she said she wasn't great at, although she enjoyed the dance training. While still in school, she began modeling professionally during her junior year. By her senior year, she was working in Los Angeles after school and eventually moved out. While Diaz has been known for decades at this point as a glamorous Hollywood actress, her background and origin aren't that different from the neighborhood rappers or athletes who find an outlet to a way out of Long Beach.

"I wasn't in CIC or PACE," she said.

Modeling was just a way out for me. I didn't think I was pretty enough, somebody else just thought I was pretty enough for me to get the fuck out. I didn't have the education; my parents didn't have money. What I had was a really strong skill set of getting along with different kinds of people, and Long Beach Poly gave me that and helped me go into the world. I thought if I could survive Long Beach, I could survive Paris.

Diaz said she was embarrassed by the modeling success she had in high school and that she kept it secret from almost everyone at the school, except a few close friends.

"I didn't want anyone to know because I didn't want anyone to think that I thought I could model," she said.

Right at the end of my senior year before I graduated, I had a **Seventeen** *magazine cover come out and everyone was like, "Wait, whaaat?" And it was the perfect timing for me because then I was out. To me it was just a way out—I wasn't going to college, I was going to graduate without any real plan in my future other than I had an opportunity that felt really big that I could see the world. That was my ambition.*

Diaz made a congratulatory video for the 2000 baccalaureate, and while she doesn't talk about Poly as often as classmates like Snoop Dogg do, she said that despite having what was at times a

162

difficult upbringing in Long Beach, the school has remained an important part of her identity.

"It's always been a real, true part of my fabric," she said. "Long Beach and Poly have been at the center of it—everything else has built out from those threads."

ON SET AT POLY

In addition to producing actors, Poly has also served as a filming location for several movies, television shows, commercials and music videos. The school has been used as the backdrop for more than ten feature films, including *American Beauty* (1999), *American Pie* (1999), *The Insider* (1999), *The Other Sister* (1999), *The New Guy* (2002), *Love Don't Cost A Thing* (2003) and *Coach Carter* (2005), and even picked up a couple notable (yet erroneous) mentions in the 2018 film *Den of Thieves*. Poly has also been used as a filming location for television shows like *Even Stevens*, *Cold Case*, *NCIS*, *Boston Legal* and others and was the site for music videos by Simple Plan, P.O.D. and Paris Hilton.

Even the Poly football team has made its way onto television screens as the subject of multiple reality television series. The 2010 team was documented on the Current TV series *4th and Forever*, and the Jackrabbits were also the subject of a 2017 documentary titled *The Machine*, produced by LeBron James's production company, UNINTERRUPTED. A USA Football docuseries also focused on the history of the program as the top producer of NFL talent in America.

In August 2019, a movie titled *Brian Banks* was released in theaters. It tells the story of the former Poly linebacker by the same name who was falsely accused of rape by a classmate. Banks was set to attend USC on a football scholarship but had his playing career derailed by the false allegation, which led to him serving nearly six years in prison and another five years on parole. Following his exoneration in 2012, Banks achieved his dream of playing in the NFL by signing with the Atlanta Falcons. Banks has also worked extensively with the California Innocence Project, the group that helped free him, and in 2014, he accepted a position with the NFL's front office, working as a manager in the football operations department.

OTHER INFLUENCES IN ENTERTAINMENT

Poly's influence in Hollywood has also been felt behind the scenes. Writer and cartoonist Ed Nofziger graduated from Poly in 1931 and had his drawings featured in national magazines like the *New Yorker*, *Parade* and the *Saturday Evening Post*. He also wrote for popular animated TV series like *Mister Magoo*, *Popeye the Sailor* and *The Dick Tracy Show*.

No Poly alum had a bigger impact in the world of animation than Marty Sklar, who after fifty years of service became the Walt Disney Company's international ambassador for Walt Disney Imagineering. During his time with Disney, he helped design iconic Disneyland attractions like the Enchanted Tiki Room and It's a Small World and headed creative development of Epcot at the Walt Disney World Resort in Florida.

Sklar joined Disney in 1956 following his graduation from UCLA and was tasked with writing marketing sales brochures for the company. Some of Sklar's earliest writing experience came as a student at Poly, where he became the editor of the *High Life* in 1951 and had his own sports column called "Sklargazing," which he discussed in his 2013 autobiography titled *Dream It! Do It!: My Half-Century Creating Disney's Magic Kingdoms*. Shortly after his hiring at Disney, Sklar became the right-hand man to company founder Walt Disney, writing speeches and other materials on his behalf.

On the day of Sklar's retirement in 2009, Disneyland honored him with a window dedication ceremony on Main Street U.S.A., where his name is still printed on a window of the city hall building. He was recognized as a Disney Legend in 2001, the equivalent of being a Disney Hall of Fame inductee, and was given the Diane Disney Miller Lifetime Achievement Award in 2016 from the Walt Disney Family Museum.

Following Sklar's passing in 2017, Disney chairman and CEO Robert Iger described his contributions to the company: "He embodied the very best of Disney, from his bold originality to his joyful optimism and relentless drive for excellence. He was also a powerful connection to Walt himself. No one was more passionate about Disney than Marty, and we'll miss his enthusiasm, his grace and his indomitable spirit."

Despite not being a star of the screen or stage, Dorothy Buffum had her own direct impact on the performing arts. Her father and uncle founded the Long Beach–based department store chain Buffum's, which had as many as sixteen locations throughout Southern California, but Dorothy quickly made a name for herself.

After marrying Norman Chandler, who would eventually become publisher of the *Los Angeles Times*, Dorothy Chandler began a life of fundraising and community organizing. Beginning with a benefit concert in 1955, she kicked off an ambitious fundraising campaign to open a performing arts center in Los Angeles. She helped raise nearly $20 million over a nine-year period, which led to the construction of the Los Angeles Music Center in 1964.

The original complex featured three venues at its site at First Street and Grand Avenue in Downtown Los Angeles: the Mark Taper Forum, the Ahmanson Theater and the Dorothy Chandler Pavilion. The Academy Awards were held intermittently in the Dorothy Chandler Pavilion a total of twenty-five times from 1969 to 1999, and the venue served as the home of the Los Angeles Philharmonic from 1964 to 2003, up until the Walt Disney Concert Hall was added to the complex. Recognizing her work in securing funding for the Los Angeles Music Center, a 1964 issue of *Time* magazine described it as "perhaps the most impressive display of virtuoso money-raising and civic citizenship in the history of U.S. womanhood."

In the theater world, 1912 Poly graduate Glenn Hughes had a tremendous impact not only as the director of the drama program at the University of Washington, a position he held for three decades, but also in theater design itself. He was instrumental in the design and construction of the Penthouse Theater, which introduced the concept of theater-in-the-round to the United States. The theater utilizes arena-style seating that brought the audience closer to the actors by wrapping seats entirely around the stage, which was centrally located in the arena.

The 172-seat Penthouse Theater was completed in May 1940 on the Washington campus and drew immediate national attention and praise. In 1949, the *New York Times* declared that Hughes was "landlord of the finest theatre in America." The theater was moved to a new location on campus but is still in use today as the Glenn Hughes Penthouse Theater.

Whether it's former Poly students or the school itself making a cameo appearance, Long Beach Poly's connection to Hollywood and the performing arts is an ongoing tradition, in all facets of show business.

19

SCHOLARS

PACE & CIC, POLY'S MAGNETS

Poly's reputation for academic excellence is buoyed by its elite magnet programs, which have not only afforded Long Beach's students access to a world-class education but also helped the school maintain its socioeconomic and racial diversity—an essential component of the Poly experience.

The roots of the PACE program can be traced back to 1975 and the efforts of Dr. Nancy Gray, who started as a French teacher at Poly in 1962. Her background made her uniquely suited to the role. A Fulbright Scholar who grew up on Native American reservations, Gray had lived in France, Mexico, Venezuela and the Arabian Peninsula prior to her arrival in Long Beach, bringing a much different perspective to the school.

"When I came to Long Beach, it was the first time I'd lived in an American city," said Gray. "I had really never lived anywhere where my race, language and ethnicity were in the majority. I thought it was perfectly normal that that was not the case."

Gray was in a unique position to not only understand the needed academic rigor of a magnet program but also carry out her charge from the PCIC—to uphold and expand on the diversity of the student body. That required talking to the parents of prospective PACE students and convincing them to believe in both the academic merits of the program and the racial harmony of the entire school, despite the reputation of the Poly neighborhood as being unsafe. "It was really a tough sell in the early years," admitted Gray. "You had to really believe in the advantages of diversity."

The first PACE graduating class in the spring of 1978. *Courtesy* Caerulea *archives.*

The sales pitch worked, and in the 1975–76 school year, the Program of Additional Curricular Experiences was born. The origin of the name is actually remarkably fitting for a collection of gifted students. In the summer leading up to PACE's launch, Gray and her newly hired faculty were struggling to come up with a name for the program. After sitting around for a few hours and coming up with nothing, Gray decided to take a different approach. "I delegated this to the students," she said. "Within thirty-five or forty minutes, they had come up with PACE."

Gray dedicated an incredible amount of time that first year, serving as head counselor to the 152 original PACE students while also teaching six classes. "That year I had 204 students on the roll," Gray recalled. "One class had so many students that some of them sat on the windowsill."

In that first year of PACE, Poly students were offered AP exams in history, biology, European history, chemistry, English literature, art history and music theory. By the program's second year, there were ninety-eight Advanced Placement tests given, with a 77 percent pass rate, earning college credits for those passing students. Less than a decade later, by 1984, Poly was offering more AP courses than any other school west of the Mississippi.

Class schedules were rigid for students, requiring them to stick to a predetermined slate of courses. "This would not have worked if we had not given the kids a schedule they had to take," Gray explained. "There was room for a few electives, but by and large they all took a basic college preparatory program. We made them stick with it. We billed PACE as a program for students who were willing to commit to a premium college admissions program."

All PACE students were required to take seven classes, instead of the standard six, and were even asked to fill out a loyalty oath on their application, in which they agreed to take all of the prescribed courses. The program gained traction quickly, and it was to the benefit of students all over Long Beach. In its fifth year, the size of the program had grown to 360 students, with half of them bused in from other high schools. In order to grow the program while PACE was still in its infancy, students from other schools were able to take PACE classes before returning to their schools for the other half of the day. It was not uncommon to see a student take PACE classes at Poly in the mornings, then finish the day at a rival high school in the afternoon. Until the mid-'90s, PACE students were even operating on a different bell schedule than the rest of the campus, creating a separation between PACE kids and the rest of the student body.

Gray spent eight years running the PACE program and saw its enrollment grow from 152 students to 445 by the time she left Poly in the fall of 1983 for a job with the school district's central office. By that point, the groundwork had been set, and PACE was on track to being among the top high school academic programs in the nation.

In the years since, PACE has built a national reputation, with more PACE students admitted to Ivy League schools and the University of California (UC) system than any other public school in the nation. One year in the early 2000s, four PACE students were accepted to Caltech, believed to be the only time the prestigious institution had accepted that many applicants from the same high school, much less a single public school academy. According to former PACE coordinator Richard Garretson, Caltech's dean of admission told him that since its inception, PACE itself had had more students accepted into Caltech than any other high school in the nation. The program isn't just about having a few standouts at the top, either. According to a 1998 article in the *Los Angeles Times*, Poly had sixty-six students accepted to UCLA, with a whopping fifty of those coming from the PACE program.

"One-third of our PACE seniors were accepted by UCLA," Garretson told the *Times*. "That is quite extraordinary."

The program still prides itself not just on college acceptances, but on retention as well. The mission of PACE is not just for students to get into college, but to excel once they arrive. Led by the large influx of magnet students into the well-respected UC system, Poly is well above the district's average rate of retention and graduation after four years on a UC campus. In the fourth year after admission into a UC school, Poly students have a retention/graduation rate north of 75 percent, easily above any other high school and the district average of just over 60 percent.

Thanks to the many Advanced Placement courses and exams offered at Poly, most PACE students enter college with plenty of college credit already in hand. Many students even have enough credits to be considered college sophomores on their first day on campus. On average, the PACE program has a pass rate of around 75 percent on all AP exams, ahead of Poly's campus-wide pass rate of just below 60 percent and the LBUSD average at around 30 percent which, of course, also includes the PACE students. That number is even more impressive considering that students often take multiple AP exams in a given year. PACE students are exposed to an AP course load in their ninth-grade year with the required AP environmental science, setting the stage for as many as six AP courses on their schedule by the time they're seniors.

Former PACE director Helene Goodman's quote sums up the renowned program's philosophy, albeit in morbid terms: "We kill them first in high school so that they feel better in college."

"PACE was always built around AP courses," said Steve Meckna, a teacher at Poly since 1989 and a member of the PACE faculty since 1991. "And this is long before these things became commonplace. So PACE was really a pioneer on that. Nowadays, the district is pushing really hard for everyone to take an AP course. To me, it's kind of funny and flattering that so much of what the district is trying to do now is what PACE has been doing since the '70s."

The program offers unique learning opportunities outside the classroom, including the chance to conduct a year-long research project with mentor physicians at UCLA and Cedars-Sinai Medical Centers. PACE was also recently selected as one of just 114 programs in the country to be part of the AP Capstone program, which awards the AP Capstone Diploma to students who pass AP Seminar and AP Research exams, along with at least four other AP exams. According to the College Board website, this honor "signifies their outstanding academic achievement and attainment of college-level academic and research skills."

Connie Loggins served as PACE counselor from 2006 until her retirement in 2019 and always intended for PACE to be about more than just academics, to create well-rounded students prepared to take on life in college and beyond.

"We are trying to transform students into leaders," said Loggins. "We want them to be trailblazers, to be the critical thinkers of tomorrow. It is the whole student—intellectually, ethically. We're trying to build character and we want them to be problem solvers and humanitarians. The foundation for that was laid a long time ago."

Loggins says she hears from colleges constantly about how involved PACE students are at their schools, speaking to the vibrance of the education students receive while at Poly.

"They're not just getting into college, they're making a difference in those environments," Loggins explained. "That's why college reps want our kids, they say 'What's in the water at PACE?' Because our kids become the movers and shakers on those campuses."

Long Beach's best and brightest have gone through the ranks of the city and the state's most rigorous public school education, housed on a comprehensive, diverse public high school campus. Traditionally, colleges and universities are the first places where many students are exposed to an array of different cultures and backgrounds, but not when you're from Poly.

"I have former students tell me all the time after their first semester of college that they don't like it as much," Loggins admitted. "They say people are so separated, they don't mingle with each other. You just become accustomed to how things are at Poly. This is a model of what it should be. That's why students can excel anywhere, because we are truly representative of what the world is."

CIC

In Gray's final year as PACE coordinator, another successful magnet program joined the fold at Poly. Beginning in the fall of 1982, Greta McGree founded the Center for International Commerce, better known as CIC.

Jackrabbit Spotlight: Connie Loggins

Long before she became the PACE counselor, Connie Loggins was a girl from the Westside of Long Beach who attended Poly High School at a turbulent time in the school's history. Loggins attended Poly in the early '70s just as racial tension in the city was spilling onto the Poly campus.

"When I went to Poly it was very diverse, and I still have friends from that time of all ethnicities," Loggins recalled. "We still consider ourselves a family to this day. We're the Poly family. There was a lot of Poly pride because there was already a dynasty that was built. Initially because of the athletics and then with PACE we became that academic power as well."

Loggins was an active member of student government as well as a Polyette during her time in high school. Though that era is remembered for the racial tensions and fighting on campus, the experience of overcoming that turmoil was an important lesson for Loggins and her classmates.

"That's a skill set that we all need. Those are life skills that are not taught, they're caught. Just by being in that environment and realizing that there's no school like ours. That's a message that needs to come down from the top."

After attending college at San Jose State and Long Beach State, where she earned her degree in community health education, Loggins returned to Poly as a career education technician in December 1990. Loggins then worked her way up as a counselor and eventually took over the PACE program in the 2006–7 school year. The PACE academy was founded shortly after her graduation from the school, but she returned to her alma mater to guide some of the brightest young minds in the city.

"It really is surreal. I truly love it," said Loggins.

I truly love not the product, but the citizens that we're sending out into the world, and I do my best to equip them and bestow the values of a true Jackrabbit. In our entryway it says "Enter to Learn, Go Forth to Serve." I tell my students, "That is your charge." To whom much is given, much is required, and our students are truly equipped to make the world a better place.

McGree graduated from Poly in 1957 and worked at the school for thirty-two years, including twenty-five running CIC, which became a nationally renowned magnet in its own right. McGree's background was in business education, one of just two women in her class to get a business administration degree at Long Beach State.

Her first job at Poly was taking over a DECA marketing class from John Fylpaa, and she got off to an inauspicious start at the school.

"Someone stole my purse the first week," she remembered with a laugh. "I was determined not to stay there—but it just got better and better. I really liked the kids and they liked me. I loved working there."

In the early '80s, the school district made her an offer of starting a business-oriented magnet program and gave her a year to put it together. She spent that year interviewing people about international trade at Long Beach's bustling port, forging relationships at the local and national level that CIC would benefit from for decades to come.

PACE had been successful in bringing top-flight academic talent to the school, but the program wasn't big enough. McGree was charged with bringing more East Long Beach and Lakewood students to Poly, specifically white students.

Greta McGree, who founded the academic magnet CIC at Poly, and George Takei, the actor who came to speak to an early CIC Japanese language class in 1983. *Courtesy* Caerulea *archives.*

"It was their last ditch effort to desegregate Poly," she said. "They wanted to bring in more white kids and not just gifted kids."

McGree, however, knew that a business program wouldn't have enough pull to get kids onto a school bus to cross into what was seen as a bad part of town, so she had an idea to make CIC an honor program like PACE, but with more freedom. Her pitch had to be successful because they had to sign up one hundred ninth graders and one hundred tenth graders in year one—there would be no run-up like PACE got to get off the ground.

"Academically we were very strong, but it was a place that allowed you to pursue other things," said McGree. "We also tried to bring in more black students and a more diverse group than PACE. We had honors and AP classes, but you didn't have to take AP classes if you didn't want to. It gave kids a chance to pick what they focused on or gave them more time to play sports or music."

CIC has often been referred to as an "athlete's magnet," with a flexible schedule that allows students to still take a year's worth of college credits in AP courses or to take a less rigorous, still honors-level curriculum. Athletes like Willie McGinest, Marcedes Lewis, Ariana Washington, Darrell Rideaux and others helped bolster that reputation.

McGree poured herself into the project, personally interviewing every applicant, looking for students with high test scores and lower grades, students that were clearly bright but didn't have a perfect transcript.

The program opened with 200 students enrolled and was focused on world finance and foreign languages, including Russian, Japanese and Chinese. By its third year—thanks in part to the inclusion of ninth-grade students at high schools starting in 1983—CIC's enrollment had doubled to 400 students and eventually rose to 700 with 150 students in each class.

Because Japanese language classes were a core component of CIC in the '80s (and still are to this day), celebrities like George Takei have done assemblies for CIC students.

"George was familiar with the Long Beach community and he would come speak to our kids," said McGree. "He would have sushi teachers come over and teach the kids about sushi preparation."

PAC-RIM

The powerhouse duo of Gray and McGree would team up to form Poly's third magnet, the Pacific Rim Business Academy, better known as PAC-RIM.

"Nancy wrote the grant in 1990 for that and I started the program and sold it and kept it going—now it's a magnet in its own right," said McGree.

Libby Huff is currently running PAC-RIM, which is still funded through the California Partnership Grant that Gray wrote, ensuring smaller class sizes, dedicated computer labs and business electives. In 2018, the program received the California Partnership Academies Distinguished Academies Award, an honor given to fewer than 2 percent of similar academies statewide that offer college prep courses, career-based education and active partnerships with local businesses.

With Poly's magnet programs in full swing, the awards, praise and academic recruitment of Poly students hit new heights. In 1991, the PACE program alone had an impressive eight students named National Merit Scholars. In 2005, *US News and World Report* featured both PACE and CIC as among the top magnets in the country. Buoyed by the success of its magnet programs, Poly has routinely been listed by *Newsweek* as one of "America's Best High Schools," placing Poly among the top 5 percent of public high schools in the country.

20

CHAMPIONS

POLY'S SPORTS PROGRAMS

Poly's athletic success is the school's most public achievement and biggest claim to fame. Sports fans across the country may not know Poly's story, but they recognize the athletes who have worn the green and gold. The school's on-field achievements were recognized in 2005, when Long Beach Poly was named the best high school athletic program in the nation by *Sports Illustrated*; in 2014, ESPN bestowed the same honor on Poly, and in 2000 the California Coaches Association voted Poly the School of the Century.

"When you look at it all together with boys and girls sports and one hundred years of history, anyone who has done high school sports for any length of time will say Long Beach Poly is the greatest high school in the history of the country for sports," said Mark Tennis, California's foremost sports historian and the editor of *Cal-Hi Sports*. "There really isn't anybody close."

Perhaps the most well-known statistic surrounding Poly is that the school has sent more players to the National Football League than any other high school, with more than seventy in its history. But what many may not know is that Poly has also produced more Major League Baseball players than any other school.

The quantity of professional athletes does not dilute the quality, either. Former Jackrabbits have gone on to be Hall of Famers, World Champions, Olympians and some of the biggest names in sports. Over a ten-year span from 2008 to 2018, a Poly alum won a world championship in the three leading American pro sports leagues. Chase Utley won a World Series with the Philadelphia Phillies in 2008, Randall Goforth won the Super Bowl with the Philadelphia Eagles in 2018 and Jordan Bell won the 2018 NBA Finals as a member of the Golden State Warriors.

Jackrabbit teams have won more than 120 CIF Southern Section championships and 37 CIF State championships, both all-time records. The school's football and basketball teams are the current state record-holders for all-time wins.

One of the reasons is legendary coaches like Don Norford, Ron Palmer, Jerry Jaso, Raul Lara, Carl Buggs, Crystal Irving and others. But the school has also been blessed with dozens of long-tenured alumni in its assistant coaching ranks. Keith Anderson has been an assistant coach for the school's football, girls' basketball and track programs and has been a part of forty CIF-SS championships and twenty-six state championships.

"I think a lot of us have been in the right place at the right time," said Anderson. "I know that what's rewarding to me is working with the kids. The last thirty years I've been able to do that, it's been my life. I'm at my place, Poly has been that place."

BASEBALL

The baseball field at Long Beach Poly isn't exactly the prototype for a sports powerhouse. For years, the outfield grass also served as a practice field for the football team and the home pitch for the girls' soccer program. On rainy days, plywood boards and pizza boxes help cover the mud puddles on the field's entrance. But the sign on the left field fence reading Gwynn Family Field serves as a reminder of the great traditions of Poly baseball. The field was dedicated in 1999, honoring a man considered by many to be the greatest hitter to ever live.

Second baseman Chase Utley concluded what is arguably a Hall of Fame career in 2018 after playing sixteen combined seasons for the Phillies and his hometown Los Angeles Dodgers. A six-time All-Star with a World Series ring, Utley's number is retired at Poly campus field, along with Tony Gwynn's.

In an earlier era, Vern Stephens would go from Poly to Long Beach City College to Major League Baseball, making his debut in 1941. He was an eight-time All-Star during his fifteen-year career in the big leagues, finishing in the Top 10 in MVP voting six times. Stephens still holds the record for most RBIs in a single season by a shortstop, driving in 159 runs in 1949.

JACKRABBIT SPOTLIGHT: TONY GWYNN

Major League Baseball Hall of Famer Tony Gwynn at the dedication of Poly's baseball field as the Gwynn Family Field in honor of him and his brothers. *Courtesy* Caerulea *archives.*

Tony Gwynn graduated from Long Beach Poly in 1977 and would go on to become a fifteen-time All-Star over a twenty-year MLB career, all with the San Diego Padres. He was the top hitter in the National League an impressive eight times, won five Gold Gloves in the outfield, amassed 3,141 career hits and was enshrined in the Baseball Hall of Fame in 2007, receiving 97.6 percent of the vote in his first appearance on the ballot.

Gwynn is one of twenty-five former Jackrabbits to play in the big leagues, with nine of those twenty-five spending more than a decade in The Show. Five different Jackrabbits have been named an MLB All-Star in their career, with a combined thirty-one All-Star Game appearances among them. Gwynn's younger brother Chris was a Major Leaguer in his own right, with ten years in the bigs, and older brother Charles Gwynn is a Hall of Famer at Cal State Los Angeles. After his playing career ended, Chris continued to make a mark in the front office, rising to become the Mariners' director of player development.

Joining Gwynn, Utley and Stephens as MLB All-Stars from Poly are shortstop Rocky Bridges (in 1958) and outfielder Milton Bradley (in 2008). Billie Jean King's younger brother, Randy Moffitt, went from Poly to a twelve-year MLB career from 1972 to 1983. The most recent Poly alum to make his MLB debut was pitcher James McDonald for the Los Angeles Dodgers in 2008. During that postseason, McDonald was on the mound for the Dodgers in the National League Championship Series and faced Utley for a rare "all-Jackrabbit" at-bat.

Poly didn't just produce MLB players, however. Poly alum Charlie Williams spent over two decades as an MLB umpire from 1978 to 2000 and made history in 1993 when he was the first African American to serve as the home plate umpire in a World Series game.

Poly alum Chase Utley closed out his tremendous Major League Baseball career just up the freeway from Poly with the Dodgers. *Photo by Stephen Carr.*

Former Jackrabbits have also had success in the scouting world, including current New York Mets SoCal area scout Glenn Walker, but none has matched the impact of legendary MLB scout Roger Jongewaard. A catcher who was signed out of Poly by the Milwaukee Braves, Jongewaard had a six-year minor-league career before transitioning to talent evaluating. He worked for a handful of big-league clubs in his forty-year career but had his longest stint with the Seattle Mariners, where he became the VP of scouting and player development. Jongewaard was instrumental in identifying superstar ballplayers such as Darryl Strawberry, Lenny Dykstra, Edgar Martinez and Ken Griffey Jr. During Alex Rodriguez's retirement speech in 2016, he thanked Jongewaard by name for drafting him to the Mariners organization.

"Roger Jongewaard is a scout's scout," Mariners president Chuck Armstrong told the *Seattle Times.* "I think he's the best talent evaluator I've ever run across in baseball."

Away from the diamond, Jongewaard's name is recognizable in the Bixby Knolls community where he and his wife, Carol, opened a family restaurant, Jongewaard's Bake N Broil, in 1965. The restaurant has become a community staple and remains one of Long Beach's most popular eateries.

FOOTBALL

Long Beach Poly is nationally regarded as a football factory. A total of more than seventy Poly alums have reached the NFL, with two or more Jackrabbits making their NFL debuts in every decade since the 1920s. A pair of Jackrabbits—Don Hill and Roy Baker—were members of the Green Bay Packers' first NFL Championship team in 1929, becoming the first of seven Poly alums to win a world championship.

Wide receiver Johnny Morris was the first Jackrabbit to be named to the Pro Bowl, earning that honor in 1960. Three years later, he won the 1963 NFL Championship with the Chicago Bears, where he spent his entire ten-year career and remains the franchise's all-time leader in receiving yards with 5,059. Willie Brown made an impact in the NFL after winning titles at Poly and NCAA titles in both football and baseball at USC. After his playing days, he returned to the gridiron as an assistant coach at USC and in the NFL with the Tampa Bay Buccaneers.

Wide receiver Gene Washington was a four-time Pro Bowler in his ten years as a player before going on to a career in the NFL front office, serving as the league's director of football operations until his retirement in 2009. He also appeared in a handful of movies and television shows during his playing career in the 1970s.

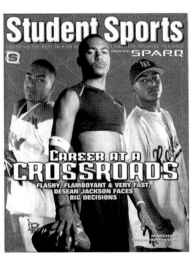

DeSean Jackson was a multi-sport standout at Poly and ultimately picked football over baseball, going on to a decade-plus career in the NFL. *Photo courtesy Student Sports.*

Safety Mark Carrier was a three-time Pro Bowl selection in the 1990s, winning Rookie of the Year for the Chicago Bears following the 1990 season. Poly has had a total of three former players win NFL Rookie of the Year. Wide receiver Earl McCullouch won it in 1968, and running back Leonard Russell went back-to-back with Carrier by winning the award in 1991.

As of the 2018 season, there were seven active Poly alums playing in the NFL, including three-time Pro Bowl wide receiver DeSean Jackson and tight end Marcedes Lewis, who was a Pro Bowler in 2010. There were two former Jackrabbits selected to the 2018 Pro Bowl, with defensive tackle Jurrell Casey

JACKRABBIT SPOTLIGHT: WILLIE MCGINEST

No Poly player has brought home more hardware than linebacker Willie McGinest, who won three Super Bowl rings with the New England Patriots from 2001 to 2004. McGinest was also a two-time Pro Bowl selection in his fifteen-year career, helping Poly's cumulative total of twenty-two Pro Bowl appearances by nine different players.

No Jackrabbit, perhaps in the school's history, has better represented all the different aspects of the school's excellence. McGinest is a Hall of Fame–caliber athlete but was also an honors student in the CIC magnet program.

"A lot of people will focus on sports, but I think what we thrive on at Long Beach Poly is we have a bunch of different programs for students," said McGinest. "You get the unique experience of having kids from all over come to a place and get the best of the best."

Like many Poly NFLers, McGinest knew at a young age he wanted to attend Poly because of the legacy of success.

"Growing up in Long Beach it's the tradition," he said.

The achievements in sports, entertainment, broadcasting, acting, academically. The people who have come through there is impressive. If you want to be the best, you always to go Poly. The funny thing is when I was playing in the NFL, all the scouts and coaches would say, "You're a Jackrabbit, huh?" It's well known throughout the league and colleges that Poly turns out good kids.

McGinest was among the very best of those kids and continues to represent the school as a host on the NFL Network, where he has frequently featured young Poly products and talked about his alma mater on the air. McGinest has also done what he can to help bring up the next generation—his Long Beach Patriots youth football team is the premier program in the city as part of the Snoop Youth Football League.

The McGinest impact at Poly isn't likely to end any time soon—not only does the national broadcaster continue to rep his high school, but his daughter Rylie also is a standout on the volleyball team and spent the summer before her sophomore year at the USA Volleyball High Performance Camp.

JuJu Smith-Schuster is one of the bright young NFL stars out of Poly; here as a senior, he poses with the mountains of NCAA recruitment letters he got. *Photo by Thomas Cordova.*

making his fourth consecutive appearance for the Tennessee Titans and second-year wide receiver JuJu Smith-Schuster getting his first career Pro Bowl nod with the Pittsburgh Steelers.

Smith-Schuster got off to a fast start to his career, becoming the youngest player in league history to reach one thousand all-purpose yards. In just his second NFL season, he also became the first player to have two offensive touchdowns of at least ninety-seven yards. He represents a proud tradition of Samoan players at Poly and was named Polynesian Football Player of the Year by the Polynesian Hall of Fame in 2017.

The other active NFL players in 2018 were linebacker Jayon Brown, wide receiver Kaelin Clay and fullback Jamize Olawale.

BASKETBALL

The Jackrabbits have also had great success on the hardwood, sending eight alums to the NBA, starting with Mack Calvin in 1976. That number leaves Poly tied for the second-most NBA players of any high school in California.

Top: Standout basketball player Tyus Edney looks to pass the ball in a 1991 photo. Edney went on to NCAA fame and is now a college coach. *Courtesy* Caerulea *archives.*

Right: Jordan Bell won an NBA championship in his rookie season with the Golden State Warriors, becoming the first Poly alum to do so. Here, Bell celebrates during the championship parade. *Courtesy of Sheldon Brown.*

The Wiley brothers, Michael and Morlon, were each second-round NBA draft picks out of Long Beach State. Morlon was actually the first player ever signed by the Orlando Magic in 1989, and he would eventually become an assistant coach with the franchise after his playing career.

Former Poly point guard Tyus Edney was a second-round pick of the Sacramento Kings in the 1995 NBA draft following a memorable career at UCLA. He was a three-time First Team All-Pac 10 selection and helped the Bruins to a National Championship in 1995. His game-winning shot against Missouri in the second round of that NCAA Tournament has gone down as one of the defining moments of the Big Dance. He was named to the UCLA Athletics Hall of Fame in 2009 and was hired as an assistant coach on the men's basketball coaching staff at his alma mater in 2017.

Poly's basketball programs have also been the beneficiary of multi-sport standouts like the Gwynns, McGinest and Marcedes Lewis. The team had a legendary coach in Ron Palmer, who won national awards while leading the Jackrabbits, and in 2007 Poly's gym was renamed the Ron Palmer Pavilion to recognize his accomplishments. His protegees have since kept the tradition going, as both Sharrief Metoyer and Shelton Diggs, Poly alums who played for Palmer, have won CIF titles while coaching Poly. Diggs's entire coaching staff is made up of alums, including decades-long assistant John Atkinson, who was a three-sport standout at Poly.

Poly's most recent NBA alum is 2012 grad Jordan Bell, who was acquired by the Golden State Warriors via trade during the 2017 NBA Draft. Bell, who was the 2017 Pac-12 Defensive Player of the Year at the University of Oregon, helped the Warriors to a championship in 2018, becoming the first former Jackrabbit to win an NBA title. As of this writing, there were fourteen former Jackrabbits playing basketball professionally or on a college scholarship, with another rising star on campus in Peyton Watson, who received a USA Basketball camp invite before his junior season.

The boys' and girls' basketball programs both lead the state of California in wins and have combined to produce six McDonald's All-Americans: Chris Sandle, Jasmine Dixon, Monique Oliver, Ariya Crook-Williams, Lajahna Drummer and Yani Clark. The boys' basketball team has twenty CIF titles to its name, while the girls' program has six state championships under head coach Carl Buggs. The Poly girls' program recently produced its first WNBA player in Arica Carter, who had a standout NCAA career at Louisville.

TENNIS

Success for former Jackrabbits at the highest levels isn't contained within just the "big three" sports, however. Poly cannot simply be defined as a football school or a basketball school. Excellence is the standard at Poly, regardless of the sport.

The most notable Poly alumnus to compete in individual sports is tennis legend Billie Jean King, who won twelve Grand Slam singles titles, sixteen Grand Slam doubles titles and eleven Grand Slam mixed doubles titles in her career. One of her defining moments as an athlete was her victory in the "Battle of the Sexes" match with Bobby Riggs in 1973, which was chronicled in the 2017 film by the same name.

Following her playing career, King emerged as a champion of gender equality and social justice. She founded the Women's Tennis Association and the Women's Sports Foundation, furthering the cause of equal opportunity for women in sports. In 2009, Barack Obama awarded her the Presidential Medal of Freedom, the highest civilian honor in the United States, to recognize her advocacy for women and the LGBTQ community.

Following in her footsteps on the tennis court was more recent Poly grad Vania King (no relation), who won her first singles title in 2006 at age seventeen. She also won a pair of Grand Slam Doubles titles in 2010, winning at Wimbledon and the U.S. Open. Vania would go on to win a World Team Tennis championship with the Springfield Lasers in 2018, defeating the Philadelphia Freedoms, a franchise owned by Billie Jean.

TRACK AND FIELD

Poly has also developed a reputation as a track and field powerhouse, winning numerous CIF and State championships and producing a solid crop of Olympians. At meets across the country, fans from all over the world know about the "Trackrabbits," even if they've never stepped foot in Long Beach. After winning the 120-yard hurdles at the inaugural CIF State Meet in 1915, Poly alum Earl Thomson would go on to set the world record in the 110-meter hurdles. Thomson would win a gold medal in that event at the 1920 Olympic Games in Antwerp, competing for his native Canada. High jumper and elite all-around athlete John Rambo followed up a terrific career at Poly with a bronze medal at the 1964 Olympics in Tokyo.

JACKRABBIT SPOTLIGHT: RON ALLICE

Long Beach Poly's storied track program not only claims some of the nation's best athletes but also some of its best coaches as well. In addition to Don Norford and Crystal Irving in recent years, Norman Barker, Leon Forman, Jim Richardson, George Wright, Mike Fillipow, Joe Carlson and Nate Bershtel have all had major success as track and field or cross-country coaches. Perhaps the finest of them all, though, is Ron Allice, who was a CIF finalist as an athlete at Poly but then made his name as a coach.

Allice, a 1958 graduate, excelled while coaching at Poly, Compton and Wilson, then went on to win eleven state titles in sixteen years at LBCC. Allice also coached at Long Beach State before his career took him to USC, where he was the director of the track and field program for two decades, winning an NCAA team title and placing in the Top 10 twenty-five times between the men's and women's teams, as well as coaching thirty-two individual NCAA champions.

Allice began coaching young, running the Long Beach Comets girls' and women's AAU program in 1964—he's still volunteering his time with athletes fifty-five years later, after an unparalleled coaching career that's produced more than 40 Olympians. In his forty-nine-year official coaching career, Allice produced 313 All-Americans, 16 Olympic medalists, 7 American record holders and 4 world record holders, while maintaining a dual meet record of 217-48-1. Allice is a member of several Halls of Fame, including the United States Track & Field and Cross Country Coaches Association Hall of Fame.

In that same year, Martha Watson graduated from Poly High as the national high school record-holder in the long jump. Shortly after graduation, Watson competed in the first of four career Olympic Games that summer in Tokyo. She was even on track to make a fifth U.S. Olympic Team before the announcement of the U.S. boycott of the 1980 Games in Moscow. Watson was a nine-time USA Indoor Champion and three-time USA Outdoor Champion in the long jump, earning induction in the National Track and Field Hall of Fame in 1987. She also won a pair of medals in the 4x100-meter relay and the long jump at the 1975 Pan American Games in Mexico City.

Andrea Anderson brought home a gold medal at the 2000 Olympic Games in Sydney, running for Team USA's 4x400 relay squad. On the men's side, Bryshon Nellum won silver in the same event at the 2012 London Olympics. Nellum was an accomplished football player as a wide receiver at Poly, but he was an elite sprinter who was named the 2007 Gatorade National Track & Field Athlete of the Year.

While attending USC in 2009, Nellum was an innocent bystander in a gang-related shooting near campus that put his career in jeopardy. Nellum had shotgun pellets in both his legs, making it difficult to walk, much less run. Through intense dedication in his rehabilitation efforts, Nellum was able to not only qualify for the Olympics but also help the Americans onto the medal stand. Because of his inspiring recovery, Nellum was chosen by his fellow athletes to be Team USA's official flag bearer at the closing ceremonies in London.

At the 2016 Olympics in Rio, Ariana Washington became the latest Olympian out of Poly as a member of the 4x100 relay team. Prior to her Olympics invitation, Washington became the first freshman to win the NCAA Championship in both the 100- and 200-meter sprints while at the University of Oregon and won eight state titles for Poly at the high school level, tied for second-most in California history.

OTHER SPORTS

Outside of the more conventional sports, Poly alums have been able to make history in other fields of competition. In 2007, less than a year after graduation, former PACE student Samantha Larson successfully climbed Mount Everest, becoming the youngest person ever to have climbed the highest mountain on each continent. She began climbing the Seven Summits with her father when she was just twelve years old and completed the Everest climb at age eighteen, also becoming the youngest non-Nepalese woman to summit Everest.

On the links, Betty Hicks was an accomplished golfer in the 1940s and '50s, hitting the scene in 1941 by winning the U.S. Women's Amateur at age twenty. That year, she was named the Associated Press Female Athlete of the Year, with Joe DiMaggio winning the men's honor. Hicks was the first Poly grad to earn that distinction, followed by Billie Jean King, who won the award twice in her career. Hicks turned pro in 1941 and would join the inaugural LPGA Tour in 1950.

JACKRABBIT SPOTLIGHT: FRANK HAWKS

Aviator Frank Hawks graduated from Poly in 1916 and would go on to be one of the most famous pilots in the world. After serving as an army pilot in World War I, Hawks would set over two hundred point-to-point records in the United States and Europe to earn the reputation as "the fastest airman in the world."

Hawks can also be credited with starting the career of one of the most famous aviators ever. On December 28, 1920, Hawks took a twenty-three-year-old Amelia Earhart on her first ever flight, and just like that, her record-breaking career was born. "By the time I had got two or three hundred feet off the ground," said Earhart, according to her website. "I knew I had to fly."

Hawks earned fame across the world for his record-setting flights, as well as his consistent presence on the news and in popular culture. He was featured in comic strips and children's books, was a spokesman for Post Cereals and even wrote books and articles promoting aviation. Hawks had a long-running radio series called *Hawk's Trail* and was the star of a fifteen-episode film serial called *The Mysterious Pilot* released in 1937.

A columnist for British magazine *Air and Airways* had this description of Hawks's career: "It seems to be a matter of general agreement in aviation circles that Frank Hawks is about the best that America has sent us. Few pilots in the world have greater claims to fame than he, yet never, I think, have I met one who was less assuming or so genuinely a 'good fellow.'"

Poly alums Samantha and Nick Jinadasa were both youth national champions in badminton who also won CIF championships while competing at the school.

Jackrabbits have also been known to break speed records, either by land or by air. In 1970, Poly grad Gary Gabelich broke the Land Speed Record (LSR) by reaching top speeds of approximately 650 miles per hour. Gabelich achieved the LSR covering both 1 mile and 1 kilometer, driving a rocket-powered racing vehicle called Blue Flame. His LSR in the mile stood for thirteen years, and his fastest kilometer record stood for twenty-seven years.

RACING, EXTREME SPORTS

In other speed-related achievements, Poly grad Tom "The Mongoose" McEwan was a highly successful drag racer in the 1960s and '70s. McEwan won the National Hot Rod Association (NHRA) U.S. Nationals in 1978, just a week after the death of his youngest son to leukemia. Perhaps his biggest accomplishment came off the track, as he and rival Don "The Snake" Prudhomme successfully struck a deal with Mattel to be sponsored by Hot Wheels. The "Snake & Mongoose" toy line helped make drag racing a household name, and Hot Wheels became the second-bestselling toy behind only the Barbie doll. In 2013, the movie *Snake and Mongoose* was released, telling the story of the McEwan-Prudhomme rivalry and their commercial success away from the sport.

Popular skateboarder Terry Kennedy went from Poly to making film and television appearances on MTV shows like *Viva La Bam* and *Rob Dyrdek's Fantasy Factory*. Kennedy, better known by his nickname "TK," also co-founded the music/clothing brand Fly Society.

Poly's athletic success has even made its way into the octagon, where 2013 Poly grad AJ McKee is one of the rising stars in mixed martial arts. McKee fights in Bellator's featherweight division and, following his victory in May 2019, holds the Bellator record for most consecutive victories with a 14-0 start to his professional career.

Afterword

GREEN AND GOLD FOREVER

One part of the Long Beach Poly culture that may or may not be apparent from the rest of this book is that Poly alums are usually a prideful and vocal group. Any Poly alum has a story about being out of state or somewhere unexpected in a Poly sweatshirt and being approached by a stranger for a half-hour conversation about the school.

Some of that is a numbers game. With 100,000 graduates, there aren't many—if any—high schools that have as many alums as Poly does floating around. But some of it is the genuine pride that comes from the knowledge of how special the school really is.

That's a fact that's known by administrators, like former Poly coach, athletic director and principal Joe Carlson. "No matter where I go, I talk to somebody and they're attached to Poly, and they're so mindful of that being a major thing in their lives," said Carlson.

It's known by world-famous entertainers like Cameron Diaz. "We had such a diversity of cultures, Samoan, Asian, Indian, Mexican, black, white, everybody's all there," she said. "Poly is Long Beach's school. It's never not been a part of my identity. It's central to who I am."

It's a fact known by star athletes like Gene Washington and Willie McGinest. "For me that's where I grew up, that's where it all started," said Washington. "Coming from that community, you can go anywhere, because you know how to get along with everyone," said McGinest.

Musicians like Harold Brown and Snoop Dogg know.

"Nothing has ever held me back from going into any kind of neighborhood," said Brown. "I never got bothered because of all my classmates. We were so integrated already. If we had issues we'd sit around the table and talk about it."

"We raise them, we breed them, then we turn them over to Poly High School to turn them into men," said Snoop Dogg. "That's what we do, we're international with this thing around here. The Home of Scholars and Champions."

Non-alums who've been around the school know how special it is.

"I went to Carson, and I don't think about it," said Keith Anderson, a longtime assistant coach at Poly. "As my kids were growing up, it was 'You're going to Poly.' It doesn't matter if they could dunk or they couldn't play at all, there was no school that could come in and buy me. It's the legacy and the history, that's something no one will ever take away from you."

Part of what makes it special is that there's a place for everyone, something Poly staffers Vincent Puth and Steve Meckna both know. "You never forget about the smaller groups; there's a huge effort to include everyone in a way that's genuine, never fake," said Puth.

"There's nothing close to a majority," said Meckna. "There's so many people with so many backgrounds, it's such a big mix. It's hard to have an 'us against them' when we're all equal."

There was a time when things could have fallen apart, a fact that former administrators definitely know.

"There was a lot of pride in the community, from white and black families that really wanted it to stay together," said HJ Green. "They really pulled together on that. Usually people abandoned those schools. I saw it happen in Tulsa. I've seen it happen all over the country."

"There's no other school like it in America," said former Long Beach Schools superintendent Carl Cohn.

At times, there's still tension, something former PACE counselor and Poly grad Connie Loggins knows:

> I've gotten a number of calls from parents saying they didn't want their son or daughter to go to Poly, but the student wanted to come because of PACE. Because they knew it was the best, it's the gold standard. Those same parents will tell me, "After having my child going there and going on the campus myself, I don't want my child anywhere else because it is such a feeling of family and cohesiveness. I have learned so much myself as a result of my child coming to Poly and I'm so glad we made that decision."

Those decisions have changed families forever. Athletic director and Poly North director Rob Shock met his wife, Brandi Brown, while they were working at the camp, and their daughters Dylan and Kendall are set to attend Poly soon.

"The school is embedded in me, there's so many people in my life because of Poly," Shock said.

The result is a school with special ties to its tradition and its community, something alum and CIC founder Greta McGree knows. "Nothing's going to happen to Poly," she said. "There's too many people that care. Long Beach is a small town in that respect, we don't go very far."

Poly grads have, of course, been all over the world, and have led the way in just about every form of entertainment and industry. Still, they seem to know where home is: every year there are dozens of third- and fourth-generation Poly students on campus. Maybe that's proof of what Poly All-American football player and Long Beach vice mayor Dee Andrews is so fond of saying: "There's two kinds of people in the world. People who went to Poly, and people who wish they did."

ACKNOWLEDGEMENTS

This book is a labor of more than three years of work, and it would be impossible to thank everyone who assisted in its creation. Please forgive any omissions.

First, a heartfelt thanks to Ben Gibson, our editor at The History Press, along with Abigail Fleming, our production editor, as well as the entire design and production team. Ben's patience and guidance during a long researching and writing process are the only reason you're holding a book in your hands.

Our eternal thanks to Billie Jean King for her encouragement and enthusiasm, as well as for agreeing to write the foreword to this book—an honor we'll never forget.

Thanks to photographer Stephen Carr for his excellent photography in this book as well as our author photo, and to Poly yearbook advisor Brett Alexander for his generosity with research materials and work space. Thanks as well to photographers Kirby Lee, Thomas Cordova, John Napalan, Art O'Neill and Sheldon Brown for their contributions.

Our thanks to the writers of the *Caerulea*, the *High Life* and other historical sources who helped us tell the story of the last 125 years in Long Beach through their own words.

A big thanks to Carl Cohn, who suggested writing this book five years ago; as you've read throughout this book, his suggestions are usually good ones.

Thanks to English teacher extraordinaire Shar Higa for her invaluable assistance proofreading and editing the book.

Thanks to everyone who agreed to share their time for an interview, especially Carl, Mayor Beverly O'Neill, Shawn Ashley, Joe Carlson, Nancy Gray, Greta McGree, Bill Barnes, Nancy Latimer, Dave Burcham, HJ Green, Johnny Byrum, Gene Washington, Bob Keisser, Mark Tennis, Jim Nowell, Cameron Diaz, Harold Brown, Don Wallace, Vincent Puth, Keith Anderson, Snoop Dogg, Steve Meckna, Connie Loggins, Chris Stevens, Jeff Inui, Samantha Lawrence, Thurman Ashley, Richard Garretson, Andy Osman, Shelton Diggs, Doc Moye, John Atkinson, Carl Buggs, Sam Dimas, Don Norford, Dave Radford, Patrick Gillogly, Keith "Slice" Thompson, Andrew Ramos, Alfie "Fresh" Reeves, Ray Porter, Rick Reyes, Jeanne Wakatsuki Houston, Willie McGinest and Matt Guardabascio.

Thanks to the principals at Poly while we were writing the book for the assistance and guidance: Joe Carlson, Victor Jarels, Diane Prince, Quentin Brown and Bill Salas. Athletic directors Rob Shock and Crystal Irving were also incredible resources, as was the vast network of Poly alums on social media who pointed us in the right direction. Thanks to Poly librarian Annasarah Ferguson for sharing workspace and archives and to *High Life* advisor Daryl Holmlund. Thanks to Sam Dimas and all the other proud Jackrabbits over the years who have collected, condensed and preserved Poly's history. It was an honor to continue your terrific work.

FROM MIKE

Thanks first and foremost to my wife, Shar, and our kiddos, Vincent and Maya, for being generous with my time. I promise this is the last book for a while.

Thanks to my coauthor, Tyler—this was a blast, let's never do it again.

Thanks to my mom and brother Matt for their abiding encouragement.

Thanks to my 562 partner in crime JJ Fiddler for his understanding while I worked on this project.

Thanks to Tyler and John Nichols for their friendship and help in promoting and selling the book.

Thanks to the Belknap family. Jessica was tragically killed in a car accident while a student at Poly. The scholarship her parents, Paul and Judy, created in her honor put me through college and is the only reason I was able to afford to become a writer afterward.

Thanks to the many teachers and librarians who've encouraged me along the way, especially Judy Haenn, Laura Leaney and Rob Pigott, three of the finest English teachers in Poly history from my decidedly biased perspective. CIC counselor Ann Valdez is probably as responsible for me graduating as I am.

FROM TYLER

I would first like to thank my coauthor, Mike, for including me in this project and guiding me along in the journey. There's no one more qualified than him to tell this story, and I'm grateful to have my hand in this project.

Thank you, Sarah, for your consistent and genuine encouragement throughout this process. It wasn't always easy, so thank you for being my person and holding me down every step of the way. Also a big thank-you to my friends and family for their support in completing this book.

Thank you to my mom for making me believe I could do anything and for being such an incredible role model. I wish I could share this book with my dad. We went to countless Poly football games when I was growing up, and though he never got to see me graduate from Poly, I know he would be "tickled to death" to read this history.

I also genuinely appreciate the inspiration and mentorship from my teachers at Poly. Especially Patrick Gillogly, who works tirelessly to inspire his students and was still able to value my spontaneous, unsolicited contributions to his class. I'm also incredibly grateful for the continued mentorship of such great administrators like Shawn Ashley, Joe Carlson and Debbie Hughes. If there's two kinds of people in the world, I'm one of the lucky ones.

INDEX

A

Academy Awards (Oscars) 14, 158, 165

Ace of Spades 99, 100, 101

Advanced Placement (AP) 89, 93, 168, 169

Alexander, Brett 94

Allice, Ron 185

Anderson, Andrea 186

Anderson, Keith 98, 176, 190

Andrews, Dee 62, 63, 65, 147, 191

ASB 26, 107, 108

Ashley, Shawn 75, 76, 80, 82, 88, 104, 105, 106, 109, 111, 120

Atkinson, John 183

B

Banks, Brian 163, 164

Barnes, Bill 60, 62, 72, 74, 78, 80, 82, 83

Bell, Jordan 176, 183

Benioff, Hugo 28

Bing, Darnell 109

Bradley, Milton 177

Britton, Barbara 159

Brooks, Mildred Bryant 122

Brown, Harold 149, 189, 190

Brown, Oscar 67

Brown, Quentin 111

Brown, Willie 62, 67, 179

Buggs, Carl 134, 176

Burcham, David 22, 23, 24, 25, 30, 41, 42, 43, 44, 45, 46, 49, 53, 54, 56, 81

Bush, Grace 17

Butler, Mary 80, 81, 83, 84

Byrum, Johnny 126

C

Caerulea 20, 27, 29, 32, 35, 36, 44, 45, 46, 59, 90, 92, 94, 108, 116, 126, 127, 152

Calvin, Mack 181

Carlson, Joe 111, 189

Carrier, Mark 179

Carter, Arica 183
Casey, Jurrell 111, 179
Chandler, Dorothy 164, 165
CIC 93, 94, 95, 97, 107, 109, 111,
　　148, 160, 170, 172, 173, 174,
　　180, 191
CIF 29, 30, 62, 63, 67, 68, 79, 92,
　　108, 132, 134, 135, 176, 183,
　　184, 187
Cohn, Carl 75, 79, 80, 81, 82, 84,
　　86, 87, 88, 96, 97, 104, 106,
　　138, 190
Collins, Mel 88, 104, 106, 111
Comus 28, 65, 151, 153

D

Daggs, Percy, III 160
Day, Laraine 159
Diaz, Cameron 95, 117, 161, 162,
　　163
Diggs, Shelton 183
Dimas, Sam 103
Dove Shack, The 143
Doyle, Clyde 22, 30
Drury, Morley 29
DuBois, Jack 74, 80

E

Edney, Tyus 183
Emi, Frank 57
Emmy Awards 14, 159
Enter to Learn, Go Forth to Serve
　　13, 47, 115, 171
Eveland, Ed 90, 91, 93, 153

F

faces (artwork on campus) 123, 124
FBI 55
flagpole 13, 41, 44, 49, 114
Fleming, Seinne 160
Ford, Lita 148
Founder's Rock 13, 114, 115
fraternities 151, 152, 153, 154

G

Gabelich, Gary 187
gangs 97, 98, 99, 100, 101, 106,
　　107, 186
Garcia, Genero 73, 74
Garcia, Robert 147
Garretson, Richard 168, 169
G-Funk 143
Girls' Athletic Association (GAA)
　　134
Goforth, Randall 176
GRAMMYS 14, 95, 111, 139, 143,
　　144, 146, 147, 148, 150
Gray, Nancy 88, 89, 90, 166, 167,
　　168, 170, 173
Green, HJ 96, 97, 98, 99, 101
Gustafson, Julia 139
Gwynn, Charles 177
Gwynn, Chris 177
Gwynn, Tony 79, 177, 183

H

Hall of Fame 31, 63, 68, 79, 115,
　　116, 117, 121, 159, 164, 175,
　　176, 177, 180, 181, 183, 185

Harnett, Jane 18, 26, 124
Hawks, Frank 187
Heflin, Van 158, 159
Hicks, Betty 186
Hicks, Howard 43, 56, 57, 59
High Life 71, 96, 116, 151, 152, 164, 194
Hilburn, Karen 101, 155
Hollywood Walk of Fame 145, 157, 159, 160
Horne, Marilyn 146
Houston, Jeanne Wakatsuki 54, 55, 56
Houston, Thelma 146, 148
Hughes, Glenn 165

I

Intercultural Fair 14, 65, 90, 91, 108, 157
International Ambassadors 90, 91, 93
Irving, Crystal 100, 134, 135
Ishimine, Joanne 160
Ivy League 14, 90, 168

J

Jackrabbits 26, 29, 62, 100, 108, 109, 117, 120, 132, 134, 135, 150, 163, 175, 177, 179, 181, 183, 184
Jackson, DeSean 111
Japanese internment 128, 160
Jarels, Victor 111
Jaso, Jerry 109, 176
Jinadasa, Nick 187

Jinadasa, Samantha 187
Jones, Spike 144, 161
Jongewaard, Roger 178
Justice, Winston 109

K

Kellogg, Keith 113, 130
Kennedy, John F. 22
Kennedy, Terry 188
Kienholtz, Edgar 32
King, Billie Jean 38, 62, 65, 67, 68, 111, 115, 132, 152, 161, 177, 184, 186
King, Vania 184

L

Lara, Raul 109
Larson, Samantha 186
Latimer, Nancy 80, 81, 82
Lewis, Marcedes 109, 173, 179, 183
Loggins, Connie 76, 117, 170, 171
Long Beach Unified School District (LBUSD) 19, 54, 71, 72, 73, 78, 79, 80, 93, 96, 104, 106, 156, 169
"Loyalty" 117, 136

M

Mack, Gwen 111
Major League Baseball (MLB) 14, 176, 177
McCowan, Walter Ray 60

McCullouch, Earl 67
McDonald, James 177
McEwan, Tom 188
McGinest, Willie 63, 79, 95, 96, 173, 179, 180, 183, 189
McGree, Greta 90, 109, 170, 172, 173, 191
McKee, AJ 188
Meckna, Steve 169, 190
Metoyer, Sharrief 183
Middough, Lorne 39, 49
Moffitt, Randy 177
Moore, George C. 33, 136
Morris, Johnny 179
Motley, Marvin 67
Mr. & Mrs. Jackrabbit pageant 119
Mulligan, Bill 66
murals 13, 42, 101, 121, 122, 123, 147

N

NAACP 71, 84
NASA 31
Nate Dogg 95, 98, 143, 144
National Football League (NFL) 14, 52, 63, 66, 109, 111, 175, 179, 180, 181
Nellum, Bryshon 63, 186
Newland, Walt 71, 72
Nguyen, Huong Tran 101
1933 earthquake 13, 14, 35, 36, 38, 39, 41, 42, 43
Nofziger, Ed 164
Norford, Don 63, 109, 176
Nowell, Bradley 95, 148

O

Olympians 29, 63, 67, 75, 134, 175, 184, 185, 186
O'Neill, Beverly 80, 101
Osman, Andy 95, 109, 138, 139, 140
Owens, Ikey 95, 150

P

PACE 88, 89, 90, 92, 94, 97, 98, 109, 111, 117, 166, 167, 168, 169, 170, 171, 172, 173, 174, 186, 190
PAC-RIM 97, 173, 174
Palmer, Ron 92, 109, 176, 183
Phillips, Neil 58, 66, 68, 115
Piercy, Wayne 96
Poly Community Interracial Committee (PCIC) 78, 79, 80, 81, 82, 83, 84, 85, 86, 87, 88, 89, 90, 91, 93, 95, 166
Polyettes 117, 162, 171
Poly North 86, 88, 96, 107, 191
Poly seal 68, 117, 119
Portia 28, 153
Prince, Diane 111
PTA 41, 49, 84, 95, 116
Puth, Vincent 97, 98, 107, 108, 149, 190

R

Radford, Dave 70
Rambo, John 67, 75, 184

Rideaux, Darrell 173
Rivera, Jenni 95, 96, 147, 148
Roosevelt, Franklin D. 54
ROTC 30, 45, 56, 62, 65, 92, 100, 116, 126, 127, 138
Russell, Leonard 179

S

Salas, Bill 111
Scarabs 28, 65, 151, 152, 153
Scholars and Champions 116, 117, 136, 190
Shock, Rob 88, 96, 108, 191
Sklar, Marty 164
Smith-Schuster, JuJu 111, 181
Snoop Dogg 95, 96, 98, 113, 143, 144, 162, 189, 190
sororities 151, 152, 153
Sphinx 28, 153
Sports Illustrated 109, 111, 175
Stafford, Jo 130, 131, 145, 146
Stanford 23, 66, 90
Stephens, Vern 176, 177
Stevens, Chris 95, 109, 139
Sublime (band) 95, 99, 148, 149

T

Takei, George 173
Taylor, Ruth Ashton 159, 160
Tennis, Mark 132, 175
Thiessen, Tiffani-Amber 95, 160
Thomson, Earl 184
Tichenor, Edna 160
Title IX 92, 132

tunnels 116, 117
Twinz 143, 150

U

UCLA 31, 138, 160, 164, 169, 183
University of California (UC) 14, 168
USC 22, 23, 29, 179, 186
Utley, Chase 176, 177

V

Vietnam War 70, 85, 86

W

Wallace, Don 73, 78, 81, 109, 153
War (band) 149
Warren G 143, 144
Washington, Ariana 173, 186
Washington, Gene 66, 179, 189
Watson, Martha 62, 67, 132, 134, 185
Wayne, John 158, 159
Weathers, Carl 113, 160
Webster, Maggie 101, 104, 155
Whipple, Fred Lawrence 31
Wiley, Michael 183
Wiley, Morlon 183
Willmore, William 17
Wilson High School 32, 33, 38, 52, 71, 99, 128, 148
World War I 30, 32, 53, 125, 126, 127, 187

World War II 52, 53, 56, 57, 58,
        59, 127, 128, 130, 131, 138
WPA 121, 122
Wright, George 109
Wright, Manuel 109
Wright, Odie 64, 72, 93

Z

Zayn 153

ABOUT THE AUTHORS

MIKE GUARDABASCIO has been covering Long Beach sports professionally for more than a decade and has had his work published in dozens of Southern California magazines and newspapers. He's the co-founder and editor of the562.org and has won numerous statewide awards for his coverage of the city. He's the author of two previous books for The History Press: *Football in Long Beach* and *Basketball in Long Beach*, written with Chris Trevino. He lives in Long Beach with his wife and children, Vincent and Maya. He can be reached on Twitter @Guardabascio or via email at mike@the562.org.

TYLER HENDRICKSON was born and raised in Long Beach and graduated from Poly's PACE program in 2007. He spent five years as a sportswriter at the *Grunion Gazette* and the *Long Beach Press-Telegram* and is currently an associate athletic communications director at his alma mater, Long Beach State University, where he earned his bachelor's in business management and his master's in sport management. He can be reached on Twitter @STylerRoth or via email at strh18@gmail.com.

JACKRABBIT MEMORIES

JACKRABBIT MEMORIES

- Fall 2015 - Ngoc first met Scott when he began his student teaching
- Fall 2017 - Scott teaches @ Poly
- Fall 2018 - Scott long·term subs for Mrs. Tram

JACKRABBIT MEMORIES

Visit us at
www.historypress.com
....